The HAPPY

The HAPPY VALLEY

A History and Tour of the Hong Kong Cemetery

Ken Nicolson

香港大學出版社
HONG KONG UNIVERSITY PRESS

Hong Kong University Press
14/F Hing Wai Centre
7 Tin Wan Praya Road
Aberdeen
Hong Kong

© Hong Kong University Press 2010

ISBN 978-988-8028-10-8

Secure On-line Ordering
http://www.hkupress.org

British Library Cataloguing-in-Publication Data
A catalogue record for this book is available from the British Library.

Printed and bound by Goodrich International Printing Co. Ltd., Hong Kong, China

Contents

Acknowledgements

The eighteenth-century writer and lexicographer Samuel Johnson once said that, 'what is written without effort is in general read without pleasure.' I count myself fortunate to have been able to combine effort and pleasure in writing this book, thanks mainly to the contributions made by the following people.

My colleagues and friends, Dr Lynne DiStefano and Dr Hoyin Lee, of the Architecture Conservation Programme at the University of Hong Kong, nagged me to write this book. Polly Hui's newspaper article about my research kept up the pressure and caught the eye of Colin Day at Hong Kong University Press. Subtle prods and timely nudges from Colin, his successor Michael Duckworth and the staff at the Press got me started and kept me going to the end.

Many others kindly shared their specialist knowledge and skills along the way. My sister, Janice, rendered the watercolour that graces the cover of the book. Dr Gary Ades of Kadoorie Farm told me all about bats. Dr Roger Kendrick and his colleagues from the Hong Kong Lepidopterist Society carried out the moth and butterfly surveys. Background information on the Japanese graves was provided by Mr Fukumitsu, Secretary General of the Hong Kong Japanese Club. Ayako Fukushima of Kyushu University translated inscriptions on the Japanese memorials and Alexandra Sauvegrain perfected my dodgy French for discussions with Père Lachaise staff.

I also learned a lot from Jason Wordie about Hong Kong's social history during one of his cemetery tours. Dr Jason Ali and Paul Harrison gave me helpful tips on identifying different stones and making repairs respectively. And, of course, the cemetery managers and staff at Père Lachaise, Glasgow Necropolis and the Happy Valley cemeteries gave me valuable insight into the challenges they face on a daily basis to manage and conserve these wonderful heritage sites.

The final word of thanks goes to Marjory, Mai, and Jasmine who were there for me from start to finish and tolerated my preoccupied moments with the patience of saints.

1 Grave Concerns

> They wandered in gardens of fragrance, and slept in the fortresses of Security . . . they were daily entertained with songs, the subject of which was the Happy Valley.
>
> Samuel Johnson[1]

To most Hong Kong residents, 'Happy Valley' is synonymous with horse-racing. This is not surprising since every Wednesday evening during the racing season, tens of thousands of punters flock to the racetrack to indulge in some serious gambling. Anyone in the vicinity on race nights cannot fail to notice the glare of the floodlights or hear the roars of the crowd reverberating around the valley. Even on Saturday afternoons, when race meetings are normally held at the Sha Tin racetrack, large numbers of people still come to Happy Valley to place their bets and, with the aid of the latest technology, watch the racing action live on a huge TV screen.

However, the name 'Happy Valley' is not derived from the fun and excitement of race days. The answer lies less than half a furlong away behind the grandstand and across the busy Wong Nei Chung Road. Parallel to the highway is an ensemble of four charming nineteenth-century cemetery gardens. This relatively untouched, tranquil and verdant landscape is a rare oasis amidst the surrounding urban development and provides a stark contrast to the clamour of the racetrack.

Fig. 1.1 Aerial view of the Happy Valley racetrack separated from the cemeteries by the grandstand, Wong Nei Chung Road and Aberdeen Tunnel approach road. Reproduced with the kind permission of the Director of Lands. ©The Government of Hong Kong SAR. Licence No. 14/2009.

In the 1800s, the name 'Happy Valley' was commonly used in Britain as a euphemism for cemeteries. The term most likely originated from the novel *The History of Rasselas, Prince of Abissinia* written by Dr Samuel Johnson in 1759.[2] The story describes the life of Prince Rasselas, son of the King of Abyssinia (modern-day Ethiopia), who lives in the 'Happy Valley' — an idyllic valley protected by impregnable fortifications from the hardships, miseries and evils of the outside world. However, when he reaches adulthood, the restless Rasselas secretly leaves the safety of his father's kingdom to explore the outside world for himself. His travels and observations convince him that there is no easy path to happiness and eventually, older and wiser, he decides to return to his homeland.

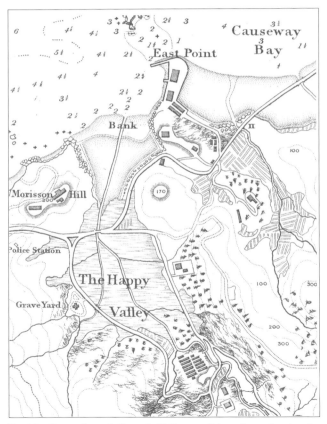

Fig. 1.2   Extract from Collinson's 1845 map of Hong Kong showing the Happy Valley and Grave Yard, now the Hong Kong Cemetery, before the racetrack was established. Wong Nei Chung Village is visible at the bottom of the figure. Reproduced with the kind permission of the National Archives.

Hong Kong's own 'Happy Valley' (formerly known as 'Wong Nei Chung Valley') owes its name to the presence of the cemetery gardens and their image as peaceful sanctuaries rather than later attempts at black humour by fun-seeking race-goers uncomfortable about having a cemetery at their backs. Despite the name, the juxtaposition of racetrack and cemeteries was considered by many to be a bad idea. One soldier living in Hong Kong in the 1850s recorded in his diary that:

> I attended several of the races, but I always considered the Race Course was in the wrong place, as the Sight of the Grave Yard generally dampened my Spirits and took all Pleasure away at these Races.[3]

A correspondent, writing in 1867 about the relationship between the racetrack and the cemeteries, noted that, 'Much discussion has arisen on what is termed the "unseemly proximity" of the one to the other. Doubtless it is a pity that such should be the case.'[4]

The Happy Valley racetrack and cemeteries date from the earliest years of the British colony. Horse-racing is first recorded in Happy Valley in 1846 although the Jockey Club was not established until 1884. The oldest and largest of the Happy Valley cemeteries is the Hong Kong Cemetery, originally called the Protestant Graveyard, and later, the Colonial Cemetery. It was established in 1845[5] in response to the urgent need for burial space to cope with the large numbers of deaths among the British garrison and civilians. In 1848, a site to the north was granted for St. Michael's Catholic Cemetery, followed in 1852 by the establishment of the Parsee Cemetery to the south. This interesting cultural landscape was completed in 1870 with the construction of the Muslim Cemetery to the north of St. Michael's. A slightly more distant neighbour, in Shan Kwong Road, is the beautifully maintained Jewish cemetery, established in 1855.

Towards the end of the 1800s, the negative feeling towards the cemeteries mellowed to some extent. Hong Kong's living conditions had improved and better sanitation meant that there were fewer decimating outbreaks of cholera, typhoid and malaria. In addition, the appearance of the Hong Kong Cemetery was being steadily transformed by the Botanical and Afforestation Department which was responsible for the landscape maintenance of parks, street trees and amenity open spaces. In 1885, a year after the Jockey Club was established, a visitor to the cemetery recorded his impressions thus:

> Leaving our rickshaws at the gate, we pass into the peaceful solitary groves, the silence of which is unbroken, save by the joyful notes of many a singing-bird . . . a carefully tended expanse of turf, with a pretty little chapel shaded with magnificent tropical trees, interspersed with beautiful flowering shrubs, and luxuriant foliage of every tint.[6]

Interestingly, the same writer also describes the surrounding landscape and notes that the racetrack across the road was 'bordered in its entire circumference with a fringe of graceful bamboo'[7] but does not venture to say whether the bamboo hedge was to screen race-goers' views of the cemetery or vice versa.

This sentiment for more ornamental planting was consistent with the prevailing trend in the West at this time to design cemeteries to function both as dignified memorial gardens as well as public parks. The first cemetery garden, built at Père Lachaise in Paris in 1804, proved popular with visitors who enjoyed strolling along tree-lined paths, admiring the craftsmanship of the stone memorials and reading the engraved epitaphs. By the mid-1800s, most British cities had established cemetery gardens of their own using Père Lachaise as a model. However, the concept of a cemetery being designed and functioning as a public park did not transpose comfortably into Hong Kong.

This is due to two fundamental reasons. Firstly, there is a profound cultural difference between the British and Chinese traditions regarding cemetery visits. In Hong Kong, the Chinese population observes two grave-sweeping festivals — *Ching Ming* in spring and *Chung Yeung* in autumn. On these public holidays, families visit their ancestors' graves and sweep off accumulated leaves, repaint the engraved lettering and pay their respects with offerings. Only the ancestors' graves are visited and it is not considered appropriate to stroll around the cemetery looking at other graves. Visits to cemeteries at other times of the year are considered to be inauspicious and avoided if at all possible.

Secondly, Chinese cemeteries in Hong Kong rarely have surplus land for extensive ornamental planting. The limited space available means that burial plots are laid out very close together. A typical cemetery is located on steep terrain, often on the urban fringe, built as a series of terraces and concrete retaining walls. There is little opportunity for providing gentle paths, sweeps of lawn or avenues of trees. To reach most graves requires a strenuous climb and nimble footwork on the narrow steps.

Although the cemetery gardens in Happy Valley were not visited to the same extent as their Western counterparts, the local wildlife took full advantage of these undisturbed habitats, enriched by the introduction of exotic flora by the staff of the Botanical and Afforestation Department over many years. In the 1890s, naturalists declared Happy Valley and, in particular, the Hong Kong Cemetery to be a paradise for butterflies.[8] Butterflies and moths are generally considered to be reliable indicators of the overall biodiversity of a site[9] and recent survey evidence suggests that the Happy Valley cemetery gardens are still some of the richest wildlife habitats in Hong Kong. Photographs taken around 1910 complement the naturalists' views and show the Hong Kong Cemetery to be a beautiful garden with handsome memorials set among mature trees, an ornamental pool and fountain, vine-covered trellises and clipped shrubs in stone pots.

Fig. 1.3   Hong Kong Cemetery circa 1910. Reproduced with the kind permission of the Hong Kong Museum of History.

In 1911, an important milestone in Hong Kong's history was established when eighteen leading members of the Chinese community petitioned the government to have their own permanent cemetery with reference to the attractive landscape of the Hong Kong Cemetery.[10] Thus, the same cemetery that had stirred discontent among visitors to the Happy Valley racetrack in the 1850s and 1860s had evolved in two generations to become a role model for establishing the Chinese Permanent Cemetery in Aberdeen.

Despite the desire of the different religious groups represented in Happy Valley and elsewhere to create distinct permanent cemeteries for their exclusive use, there has been considerable hybridising of character within each cemetery. This blurring of the boundaries between different religions and their funeral icons can be seen in a number of ways and is a reminder of Hong Kong's cultural diversity.

Although the Hong Kong Cemetery was generally understood to be for the burial of European Christians only, for various reasons this exclusivity has not been enforced consistently and their memorials are in some places intermingled with those of Japanese and Chinese nationals. In the Chinese Permanent Cemetery in Aberdeen a few memorials show an interesting juxtaposition of religious and cultural icons. For example, a Chinese Christian has selected a Celtic cross as a memorial, with a flower-like emblem in the centre rather than the standard knot pattern. Elsewhere, a traditional armchair-shaped Chinese grave has a carved dragon motif alongside an angel. Another grave has sculptures of both a Chinese lion and a Western lion. In the Muslim Cemetery in Happy Valley, it is common to find memorials with inscriptions in three languages: Arabic, Chinese and English, suggesting the deceased were truly cosmopolitan in attitude and lifestyle.

Fig. 1.4   Selection of cross-cultural icons in the Chinese Permanent Cemetery in Aberdeen

Another curiosity is that the Hong Kong, Parsee and Jewish Cemeteries all have a stone fountain laid out in the same pattern; a central square with semi-circular bays on each side. This motif is also found in many Islamic fountain, paving and even carpet designs throughout the world. What do these different religions have in common with the fountain design in three Happy Valley cemeteries? In the Bible (Genesis, chapter 2, verse 10) it states that, 'A river watering the garden flowed from Eden, and from there it divided; it had four headstreams.' The Happy Valley fountain designs are intended to represent the rivers flowing out of Eden to the four corners of the world. The images portrayed in the book of Genesis pre-date divisions between the Islamic and Christian faiths and are therefore common to both.

Fig. 1.5   Hong Kong Cemetery fountain

Fig. 1.6   Parsee Cemetery fountain

Fig. 1.7   Jewish Cemetery fountain

In recent years, heritage tours to the Happy Valley cemeteries have become more popular and attract both Western and Chinese visitors. Local historian Jason Wordie leads tours from time to time and gives insightful talks on Hong Kong's social history with reference to the lives and works of famous people buried in the cemeteries. This interest in the heritage value of the Happy Valley cemeteries is the most recent phase in the gradual change of attitude towards the Western cemetery garden concept in Hong Kong. The main catalyst for this change began as far back as the late 1800s when Western cemetery managers introduced more ornamental planting to cemeteries to enhance their appeal as public parks. The accolade paid by the Chinese community to the Hong Kong Cemetery's landscape character in 1911 confirmed that the cemetery had made a successful transition from a Western graveyard to a beautiful cemetery garden with cross-cultural appeal. Two world wars and almost a century of rapid urban growth later, Dr Solomon Bard, in his study of military graves and monuments for the Antiquities and Monuments Office, remarked that the Hong Kong Cemetery was:

> Still a pleasant and tranquil spot, in spite of the high-rise buildings, the flyovers, and ever-present noise of the rushing traffic; a place where an hour or two can be spent in quiet and thoughtful meditation.[11]

Fig. 1.8   Present-day view of the Hong Kong Cemetery

Bard also noted in his 1991 study the need for a pro-active conservation plan for the Hong Kong Cemetery.[12] Years of neglect have taken their toll on many of the memorials and, to date, nineteen years after Bard's comments, the government departments responsible for the upkeep of Hong Kong Cemetery, and heritage conservation in general, have not formulated a heritage conservation plan. Sadly, as each year passes, memorials continue to fall and break, inscriptions become less distinct and irreplaceable records of Hong Kong's history are lost. Although the Happy Valley cemeteries are the oldest and most intact historic gardens in Hong Kong, they are not protected by any statutory conservation legislation.

This book is written in response to this predicament and has two main objectives. Firstly, it aims to nurture the current impetus of rediscovering the Happy Valley cemetery gardens as valuable public open spaces for meditation and quiet recreation. Secondly, it establishes the heritage significance of the cemeteries, particularly the government-managed Hong Kong Cemetery, and highlights the need for their sensitive conservation.

Finding the correct balance between these two objectives requires a deft touch and a sound understanding of the dynamic and often subtle interactions between the man-made and natural heritage resources that have evolved in the cemeteries over the last 165 years. The following chapters trace the origins of the cemetery garden concept from early nineteenth-century Europe, its evolution and eventual introduction to Hong Kong and conclude with suggestions on how the valuable built and natural heritage resources in the Hong Kong Cemetery can be better protected.

2 Origins of the Cemetery Garden

Skeletons protruding from churchyard ground could be seen by passersby, and pressure from the two thousand bodies in Cimetière des Innocents had broken through an adjacent apartment house wall, spewing corpses into its basement.

Culbertson and Randall[1]

The quotation at the head of this chapter describes the macabre scenes and disgraceful conditions of Paris graveyards in the late 1700s that caused a widespread public outcry. The problem was not unique to Paris. Gross overcrowding of urban churchyards throughout Europe was common due mainly to the effects of the Industrial Revolution. New industries in and around towns and cities attracted and exploited country-folk seeking better jobs and living conditions. At first, the rapid urban growth was unplanned and it is not surprising that during this era of 'dark Satanic mills'[2] the well-documented unsanitary conditions for the living were exacerbated for the dead. In France, prior to the Revolution (1789–99), Christian denial of burial to criminals meant their remains were simply thrown into the town dump with household trash and excrement.[3]

Initial response to the graveyard scandal in Paris was to ban further burials in existing churchyards and transfer the surplus bodies outside the city gates to a labyrinth of disused mines and underground limestone caverns, commonly known as the 'Catacombs'. It is estimated that the remains of over six million Parisians were interred in this subterranean ossuary. However, this impersonal manner of burial and memorial was not a lasting solution and it was clear a radical approach to the burial of the dead would have to be devised.[4]

The French Revolution provided a catalyst for widespread social change and in this context of renewed civic pride the concept of the cemetery garden was set to flourish. Attractive and hygienic cemetery gardens were considered to be symbols of government competence and efficiency and represented a new respect for the dead. Criminals were now afforded proper burial and the bodies of the deceased were no longer regarded as garbage.[5]

Père Lachaise, Paris

Churchyards are usually no more than one acre (0.4 hectares) in size and generally located next to churches. By contrast, cemeteries are much larger tracts of land, 10 acres (4 hectares) or more, normally located outside the urban area. Church law applies to churchyards but not cemeteries, although cemeteries may be partly or wholly consecrated. The new generation of Paris cemeteries was proposed for the city outskirts. One of the first was located on Mont Louis, a hill to the east of the city on a site originally occupied by a Jesuit hospice. Nicholas Frochot, Paris' first Napoleonic Prefect, initiated the cemetery project. Frochot persuaded the Baron family, who had acquired the site in 1771 and had since seen their estate destroyed during the Revolution, to sell for a very low price. A leading architect of the day, Alexandre-Théodore Brongniart, was commissioned and the cemetery was promptly open for business on 21 May 1804. Initially, the new cemetery was known as 'Cimetière de l'Est' (East Cemetery) but soon became known as 'Père Lachaise' in memory of one of the former Jesuit community, Father Francois de La Chaise d'Aix, who had been Louis XIV's confessor.[6]

Brongniart's design made full use of the dramatic landscape by building a new entrance at the foot of the hill on a central axis with a series of winding and linear carriage paths connecting the lower valley around the escarpment to the upper plain. This combination of regular with irregular forms was intended to create a more formal, polished landscape in a limited central area near the Chapel and a less formal, densely planted, park-like landscape in more peripheral areas.

Fig. 2.1   Views of avenues in Père Lachaise Cemetery

Business was rather slow at first because the cemetery was located on the outskirts of the city. To 'prime the pump' Frochot shrewdly persuaded the municipal authorities to rebury Molière and La Fontaine, as well as relocate the tomb of the famed lovers Abélard and Hélöise in Père Lachaise.[7] This gave the cemetery instant status with the rich and famous and affirmed the government's dedication to improving the image and conditions of the city. By now, the main avenues had distinctive planting: limes along the central esplanade and chestnuts along the grand transverse avenue with poplars and acacias along connecting looping paths. As intended, Brongniart's Romantic-inspired design soon became more than just a cemetery. It was also an open-air museum and grand memorial garden where families would stroll at weekends and society's notables, past and present, could be noted.

Fig. 2.2   Contrasting memorials in Père Lachaise: (left) the first relocated memorial to the famed lovers Abélard and Hélöise, 1804, and the memorial to Oscar Wilde almost a century later

A cross-section of some of the other famous 'residents' of Père Lachaise include the composers Bizet, Chopin and Rossini, scientist Claude Bernard, American writer Gertrude Stein, novelists Honoré de Balzac and Marcel Proust, French popular singer Edith Piaf, opera singer Maria Callas, Moulin Rouge dancer Jane Avril, impressionist painter Camille Pissarro, comic dramatist Jean-Baptiste Moliere, jazz violinist Stephane Grappelli, and actor Yves Montand. One of the most popular graves with visitors is that of Irish novelist, poet and playwright Oscar Wilde. It is common for admirers of Wilde to leave a lipstick kiss mark on the headstone as a sign of respect.

The grave of the French journalist Victor Noir is also a big crowd puller. Noir was killed by Pierre Napoleon Bonaparte with whom he had been discussing terms for a duel with Paschal Grousset. The grave is marked by a lifelike bronze statue of Noir laid on its back, made all the more eye-catching by the bulge in the trousers suggesting that he was well-endowed. Placing a flower in his top hat and rubbing the genital region of the statue is said to increase fertility. Judging by the high polish on this particular part of the sculpture, it still seems to be a popular tradition. In 2005, a security fence was erected to prevent people from touching the statue. However, there were loud protests from local women visitors and the fence was taken down.

The most visited grave is that of American Jim Morrison, former singer-songwriter of the rock band *The Doors*. Over the years, fans have covered Morrison's grave with graffiti, signatures or lipstick kiss marks and often leave a pack of cigarettes instead of flowers on the headstone. In the past, it was necessary to post a full-time guard at Morrison's grave to stop further defacement and help disperse crowds of sightseers.

Père Lachaise is definitely not a depressing place to visit. Quite the contrary, a trip to the cemetery is like taking a stroll through history, rubbing shoulders (and other body parts) with the famous personalities that have shaped history. After two hundred years of operation the cemetery has over seventy thousand permanent residents and is still the most popular in Paris for those who can afford the high tariffs. At 110 acres (44 hectares) it is the largest park in the city, attracts around two million visitors annually[8] and is home to several hundred feral cats.

> At this peaceful site, amid trees and flowers,
> Sorrows and laments come to cry their tears;
> Here they can find a sympathetic shade;
> Death hides from their eyes its hideous scythe,
> As it spreads its subjects throughout a vast garden;
> For the home of the dead has become the new Eden.
>
> (Written in French on a terrace wall, Père Lachaise, Paris 1813)

Glasgow Necropolis: The Scottish Père Lachaise

Père Lachaise set the standard for subsequent cemeteries throughout Europe and was much praised by Britain's leading cemetery designers. In Britain, prior to the nineteenth-century cemetery movement, almost all burials were in churchyards. Recycling of graves had been a long-standing tradition. When new graves were needed, bones from the oldest graves were removed to an ossuary to make space. This relatively sustainable system worked well so long as sufficient time was allowed for proper decomposition. However, the grave recycling interval reduced steadily as the urban population swelled and pressure on limited burial space increased. The Church of England exacerbated this situation by having a vested interest in the status quo as it received a fee for each burial within churchyards.[9]

Dissent towards the restrictive Church of England burial system and unhealthy conditions of the overcrowded churchyards was strong among the new Protestant religions, particularly Methodists. The Protestants were predominantly middle-class and relatively wealthy. They admired the lifestyle of the landed gentry and their picturesque country estates as a setting for family tombs. So much so that establishing attractively landscaped private burial grounds, unattached to the Church of England, became a religious cause of the Protestants.

The first British non-denominational cemeteries were established by Joint Stock companies in Norwich (The Rosary in 1821), Liverpool (Liverpool Necropolis in 1825 and St. James Cemetery in 1830) and by a Merchants' House in Glasgow (Glasgow Necropolis in 1832). Of these great city cemeteries, the Glasgow Necropolis is generally regarded as being the finest.[10]

> There is no cemetery in Britain as spectacular as the Glasgow Necropolis for it is literally a city of the dead on its site beside the cathedral. It provides a unique architectural and townscape experience, of almost unparalleled magnificence outside Italy.[11]

The cemetery founders had visualised the Glasgow Necropolis as being a Scottish Père Lachaise where attractive planting would complement the tombs and provide visual relief to the smoke-blackened city churchyards. Glasgow was one of the leading industrial cities in Europe in the early 1800s. The rapid population growth overwhelmed the city's basic water supply and sanitation infrastructure. Cholera and typhus epidemics were common and in the 1830s over five thousand people were dying each year. Urban church graveyards could not cope with the demand and were soon in a disgusting condition. A guide to Glasgow Cathedral and the Necropolis in 1843 referred to conditions in the Cathedral graveyard, before the Necropolis was built, as 'revolting to human nature and . . . destructive to the health of the living'.[12]

Members of the new middle or merchant class, driving the industrial economy, were keen to avoid such epidemics and desired better living conditions. They also sought the means to display their success and have their achievements remembered for posterity. The Merchants' House that established the Necropolis was, at that time, an extremely powerful and influential committee of prominent tradesmen with jurisdiction over the finances of many public services, such as the police force, roads and street lighting. The Merchants' House had the primary functions of promoting fair trade as well as charitable works, e.g., providing pensions to widows and orphans.[13] Therefore, it is perhaps not surprising to discover that, although the concept design for the Necropolis was born partly from a desire to emulate the grand country estates of the landed gentry, almost all of the monuments are erected in the memory of ordinary folk who made their wealth by their own hard work.

A vision for the design of the Necropolis came from the Chamberlain of the Merchants' House, John Strang. His book, *Necropolis Glasguensis with Observations on Ancient and Modern Tombs and Sepulture*, published in 1831, was a treatise on the veneration of human remains and burial rites throughout the world. Strang grasped the opportunity to transform the fear and horror of the typical Glasgow graveyard into a source of civic pride by means of a well-designed cemetery garden. Recording his impressions of Père Lachaise Cemetery as a model for the Glasgow Necropolis he wrote:

> All the disagreeable sensations which are here coupled with a churchyard are dispelled by the beauty of the garden, the variety of its walks, by the romantic nature of its situation.[14]

The setting chosen for the Necropolis was a partly quarried hill, known as Fir Park. This high ground, beside the Cathedral, still provides a superb view across the city. The main entrance is dominated by a handsome, single-span sandstone bridge, completed in 1833. Known as the 'Bridge of Sighs' (alluding to the 'Bridge of Sighs' in Venice) this is the route of funeral processions and provides a symbolic link between the lively bustle of the inner city and the eternal peace of the cemetery. At the end of the bridge, the entrance to the Necropolis is highlighted by an ornamental stone façade. Behind this wall it was intended to provide catacombs extending far into the hill. Catacombs were considered to be necessary to foil body snatchers who would dig up freshly buried corpses and sell them to medical schools for dissection. With the passing of the 1832 Anatomy Act, which expanded the legal supply of medical cadavers, grave robbing was brought virtually to an end and the plans for the catacombs at the Necropolis were abandoned.[15]

Fig. 2.3   Bridge of Sighs with the John Knox memorial (tallest obelisk on the skyline)

The design for the Necropolis was decided by a competition arranged by the Merchants' House. A panel of judges decided that the ideas from the best five designs should be combined and that the work should be carried out under the supervision and management of the well-respected local landscape gardener, George Mylne.[16] The Necropolis was laid out on a grand scale based on Père Lachaise. Rows of tasteful and exquisitely carved memorials were set in terraces of lawn, subdivided by gently curving paths and lined with elm, plane, poplar, sycamore and oak trees. Much of the Necropolis architecture was designed by local architects John Bryce, David Hamilton and his son James. Similarly, many of the larger memorials were created by renowned architects and sculptors of the day, including Charles Rennie Mackintosh and Alexander 'Greek' Thomson. Indeed, some of the monuments are better known for their designer than the commemorated deceased.

The most visually striking monument is that of John Knox, the famous Calvinist religious reformer. A bronze statue of Knox stands on top of a 20-metre high stone column near the entrance to the Necropolis gazing down sternly upon visitors. With similar Calvinistic discipline, the Merchants' House took great care to protect the reputation of the Necropolis and ensure a high standard was maintained. All new designs for memorials and inscriptions had to be submitted for approval. In particular, memorials erected near the John Knox monument were scrutinised by the cemetery architect David Hamilton to prevent construction of anything considered to be in bad taste.[17] These management strategies paid off handsomely. Prominent visitors, such as Queen Victoria and Prince Albert during a visit in 1849, expressed their delight at the sight of the cemetery.[18]

Fig. 2.4   Views of the Glasgow Necropolis

Loudon's Law

Another great admirer of cemeteries like Père Lachaise and Glasgow Necropolis was the Scot, John Claudius Loudon — one of the foremost proponents of the cemetery garden in Britain during the nineteenth century. Loudon was a horticulturist and prolific writer on all matters of farming practice as well as the design and management of public gardens and cemeteries. In his books and articles on cemetery design Loudon describes in exhaustive detail everything from the optimum method of digging a grave to the ideal species of trees and shrubs to plant. Loudon admired the dignity of cemeteries like Père Lachaise and Glasgow Necropolis that performed the dual role of memorial garden and public open space. Loudon's book *On the Laying out of Cemeteries*, published in 1843, had a lasting and widespread influence on the layout and plant selection in nineteenth-century cemetery design. It was the first English language book on the subject and Loudon summed up the importance of this new concept of cemetery gardens thus:

> Churchyards and cemeteries are scenes not only calculated to improve the morals and the taste, and by their botanical riches to cultivate the intellect, but they serve as historical records.[19]

The earliest cemetery gardens were inspired by the desire to create a memorial garden similar to a country estate landscape, i.e., sweeps of lawn, serpentine paths, large copses of trees and eye-catching architectural features, with a chapel as a substitute for the mansion house. However, Loudon scorned this imitation of the English landscape garden in some British cemeteries.[20] Instead of creating copses of naturalistic broadleaf woodland, Loudon advocated the use of evenly distributed upright conifers, arguing that a regular grid system allowed the most rational layout of memorials and made it easier for visitors to find individual graves. These ideas and his promotion of the cemetery as an educational, contemplative and dignified environment were well-received by Victorian society. Most cemetery gardens follow one or the other approach in their layout, or even a combination of the two. Comparison of the two styles is best illustrated in engravings, shown below, prepared by Loudon of the South Metropolitan Cemetery at Norwood in Surrey.

Loudon wanted cemeteries to have a clearly distinguishable landscape character. For example, his preference for slender conifers with dark evergreen foliage created a sombre atmosphere and visual image that could not be mistaken for anything else in the English countryside.[21] This aesthetic ideal complemented the practical aspects of planting evergreen conifers that cast less shadow, allowed better drying of the ground and speeded up the decomposition process. Furthermore, clearance of fallen leaves from deciduous trees in winter creates additional maintenance work. Although not specifically stated by Loudon or his commentators, it is interesting to note from the South Metropolitan Cemetery illustrations how similar the tall slender conifers are to the stone monuments, further reinforcing the image of a cemetery landscape Loudon promoted.

Fig. 2.5   Loudon's image of the South Metropolitan Cemetery planted in the pleasure ground style. Reproduced with the kind permission of Ivelet Books.

Fig. 2.6   Loudon's image of the South Metropolitan Cemetery planted in the cemetery style. Reproduced with the kind permission of Ivelet Books.

To reinforce his design arguments, Loudon referred to contemporary examples of cemeteries in Turkey where cypress trees were traditionally planted and in China where he remarked that trees of various forms and character were traditionally planted.[22]

These references by Loudon to cemetery design in the East need to be qualified. Upon closer examination they, in some respects, appear to contradict rather than reinforce Loudon's arguments. For example, the Chinese burial grounds quoted by Loudon included a variety of broadleaf tree species including willows. Willows (*Salix*) with their 'weeping' form were a popular choice for planting in early Western cemetery gardens to represent mourning. However, they soon fell out of favour as they are typically associated with wet ground conditions and, as Loudon demonstrated, cemeteries are ideally located on gravelly, well-drained soils.[23]

Upright conifers, typically Juniper (*Juniperus chinensis*) or Buddhist Pine (*Podocarpus macrophyllus*), are common features in modern Chinese cemeteries in Hong Kong. Is the similarity between Loudon's nineteenth-century design principles and twenty-first-century Chinese cemetery landscaping a coincidence or by design? Although Loudon travelled widely throughout Europe and would likely have been exposed to the prevailing nineteenth-century interest in Oriental artifacts, it is not recorded that he visited China.

Loudon's references to nineteenth-century burial grounds in China appear to have been selected to illustrate the traditional use of well-drained hillside locations for cemeteries rather than the use of upright conifer trees. This suggests that Western and Eastern cemetery designers arrived at the same conclusion independently. That is, the best sites for cemeteries are well-drained hillsides instead of productive, low-lying farmland and that slender, evergreen trees which are drought-resistant, take up less space, and cast little shadow are the optimum choice.

Loudon's Turkish examples have even more fundamental contradictions. Like the Garden of Eden to Christians, the garden is central to the Muslim vision of paradise. The Turks have a tale to explain the importance of gardens to their faith. A famous holy man, Sheikh Hasan Efendi, was asked at a religious gathering whether any Muslim could be certain of going to paradise when he died. Hasan replied by asking if there were any gardeners present. When one member of the congregation stood up, Hasan pointed to him declaring that the gardener will go to heaven. In response to the resulting hubbub he explained that according to the hadiths (the oral traditions of the prophet Muhamad) people will do in the afterlife what they most enjoy doing on earth. Since all flowers belong to heaven, gardeners will surely go to paradise to continue their work.[24]

Thus, even during the austere Ottoman Empire, pious Muslims regarded flowers with reverence and often wore blooms in their turbans. Of all the flowers in the Muslim garden the tulip with its vibrant colours was regarded as the holiest. In Arabic script the letters that spell *lale*, 'tulip' in Turkish, are the same as those that form *Allah*.[25] Loudon himself notes that although Turkish cemeteries were typically planted with sombre cypress trees, individual graves were usually adorned by planting flowers on top.[26] This Turkish penchant for floral embellishment in life and in death is an interesting contrast to the more sober tones advocated by Loudon who was strongly opposed to planting flowers in cemeteries. He believed that the regular turning over of soil to maintain flower beds would spoil the sense of repose that should permeate a cemetery.

Loudon's strict layout and planting design principles were highly influential and widely adopted in nearly all British public cemeteries formed after 1850.[27] Grave plots were typically laid out in lawns either on a geometric grid or a neat patchwork of geometric units within a framework of gently curving tree-lined roads, paths and terraces. The selected trees were mainly coniferous with the main avenues supplemented by highlight planting of specimen trees or topiary. Loudon only designed three cemeteries himself — Abbey Cemetery in Bath, Southampton Cemetery and Histon Road Cemetery in Cambridge. Interestingly, only the latter (opened in 1843) exhibits his innovative ideas most faithfully.

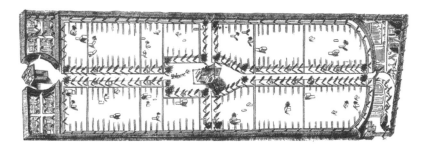

Fig. 2.7   Loudon's design for Histon Road Cemetery in Cambridge. Reproduced with the kind permission of Ivelet Books.

Histon Road Cemetery was laid out in a simple rectilinear form divided into four equal areas of lawn. A lodge house was built at the main entrance for the cemetery curator and a funeral chapel at the heart of the site where the two access roads intersected. The central road was bordered by an avenue of European Black Pine (*Pinus nigra*). This species was preferred by Loudon for its dark and solemn air and suitability for pruning into slender columnar shapes. Some cedars of Lebanon (*Cedrus libani*) were proposed as special features at the junction of the access roads, near the chapel. The slightly elevated terrace and footpath that ran around the cemetery perimeter were bordered by Irish yews (*Taxus baccata Fastigiata*) on the inside and Holly (*Ilex*) on the outside to create an effective boundary hedge. The widths of the central road and turning circle around the chapel were designed to accommodate a hearse drawn by four horses.[28]

In the late 1870s, Loudon's ideal model for cemetery design came under attack from landscape professionals and cemetery superintendents who were keen to introduce a broader spectrum of planting. Too many conifers were considered to be depressing and a more uplifting style of planting was sought. Deciduous trees began to dominate cemetery designs and oaks, elms, limes, maples and planes were commonly chosen for avenue planting. By the turn of the century, every aspect of horticulture common in public parks, e.g., potted plants, flowerbeds, and rock gardens, could be found in cemeteries as well.[29]

One practical disadvantage of evergreen conifers that Loudon seems to have played down is that deciduous trees are able to shrug off their grimy, dust-laden leaves each autumn and are rejuvenated with fresh foliage in the spring. For example, the Scots pines that once occupied Fir Park, the former site of the Glasgow Necropolis, all died due to the increased pollution from the city's coal-fired industries in the early 1800s and were replaced with hardier broadleaf trees when the cemetery was established.[30]

The new generation of cemetery gardens brought a dignity to death and a new civic pride and self-confidence to the city as a whole. Because the burial lots were typically sold in perpetuity, people were more willing to spend money on the headstones, sculptures and engravings. In the Necropolis, the legacy of this investment of money and effort in memorial design is a unique, tangible record and representation of the art and architecture of Victorian Glasgow. The wording of inscriptions, use of different kinds of stone, choice of icons and ornamentation, all reflect the fashions, social trends and religious beliefs of the day.

As described above, the main catalyst for the cemetery garden movement was the public outcry in the late 1700s and early 1800s against the sordid living (and dying) conditions in the industrial cities of Europe. A century later, a second public outcry began to be heard. In Paris, Père Lachaise Cemetery had become encircled by urban expansion and city planners wanted to clear the site for residential and commercial development. The plan was to build a mega-cemetery several kilometres outside the city, linked by a railway to facilitate funerals. However, Père Lachaise had, by then, become one of the city's most popular public parks. The people of Paris protested, their slogan being, 'Without a cemetery, there is no city.'[31] Perhaps fearing another revolution, the city government backed down and Père Lachaise was allowed to rest in peace.

Why the city planners contemplated redeveloping Père Lachaise, may have been partly due to the speed at which the cemetery was filling up. One of the main attractions of the cemetery garden concept was that the burial plots were permanent. This encouraged a high standard of memorial design and maintenance. On the other hand, once the burial plots were all sold, the flow of income to the private enterprises managing the cemetery started to run dry. The Merchants' House faced a similar problem managing Glasgow Necropolis. By the late nineteenth century, two final extensions had been added to the north and south-east, doubling the size of the cemetery to 38 acres (15 hectares). These extensions were never as popular as the original portion surrounding John Knox's monument and the cemetery went into a prolonged decline.[32]

Throughout Britain, many cemetery joint stock companies went bankrupt and the cemeteries became choked with weeds and vines. Often, local authorities had to take over responsibility for their maintenance using public funds. Understandably, such private enterprises soon gained a bad reputation and were viewed with suspicion. The Merchants' House eventually gave the Necropolis to the Corporation of the City of Glasgow in 1966 with a one-off payment of £50,000 to help with its upkeep.[33]

Inevitably, local authorities looked for ways to minimise the cost of maintenance and repairs to the cemeteries now in their charge. A common solution was to grass over the high-maintenance flower beds and remove obstructions such as benches and grave surrounds to facilitate mechanical mowing.[34] As is often the case with lower standards of maintenance and supervision, private cemetery gardens that had become overgrown, or those managed by local authorities on limited budgets, became soft targets for vandals who pushed monuments over or defaced them with graffiti.

This sorry state of affairs continued throughout the 1900s until, in the late 1970s, a third public outcry started to be heard calling for action to prevent further damage by vandalism and neglect. The Victorian Society identified a number of prominent cemeteries in Britain that needed protection, including London's Abney Park, Kensal Green and Highgate; the latter being advertised on the London underground using poignant images of marble angels overgrown with ivy. Subsequent studies by the Cemetery Research Group (funded by the Economic and Social Research Council) noted that most cemeteries have significant heritage value and recommended that, instead of concentrating resources into conserving a handful of the oldest and most famous company cemeteries, it would be more appropriate to take a broader approach and seek to understand and promote protection of privately and publicly managed cemetery landscapes as a whole — even those still in operation.[35]

This approach acknowledges that cemetery gardens were designed to function as both memorial gardens and public open spaces. Although under stress from financial constraints and occasional anti-social behaviour, historic cemetery gardens like Père Lachaise and Glasgow Necropolis are wonderful heritage resources — museums of art, architecture and social history as well as botanical gardens and nature reserves. One of the joys of visiting Glasgow Necropolis is to look up from reading a headstone inscription and come face to face with wild deer that roam round the fringes of the cemetery.

Halfway around the world, the Hong Kong Cemetery also holds surprises for the visitor, such as spotting a roost of bats hanging overhead in a palm tree, or finding a bird nesting in the crook of a marble angel's arm. Introduced 165 years ago by the British to a fledgeling colony, this cemetery garden has evolved in parallel with its European counterparts and today boasts a rich collection of built and natural heritage resources. No other urban public open space can offer this kind of experience. Making the effort to understand and protect such sites will be well worthwhile and getting the balance right between conserving the memorials and protecting the natural wildlife habitats will be a rewarding challenge.

3 The Rise and Fall of the Hong Kong Cemetery

A garden cemetery and monumental decoration afford the most convincing tokens of a nation's progress in civilisation and in the arts.

John Strang[1]

In the early nineteenth century, European cemetery gardens tended to bear a resemblance to country estate landscapes with naturalistic copses of woodland, serpentine paths and sweeping areas of lawn. From the mid-nineteenth century onwards, many cemeteries adopted a more 'Loudonesque' approach of simple and efficient grid layouts. However, the differences between the two styles of cemetery garden design were not necessarily clear-cut and many cemeteries had elements of both. Furthermore, Loudon's design principles were interpreted according to prevailing fashions, local cultural traditions and personal tastes of cemetery managers and designers. How were these Western cemetery design principles applied in the new British colony of Hong Kong and, in particular, to the Hong Kong Cemetery in Happy Valley?

The rise from graveyard to cemetery garden

In the early years of the British Colony of Hong Kong, the Royal Engineers were responsible for construction of the basic infrastructure such as roads, culverts and bridges. Therefore, it is most likely that the land granted by the Surveyor General for the Hong Kong Cemetery in Happy Valley (formerly called the Protestant Graveyard then the Colonial Cemetery) was also formed by the Royal Engineers. Loudon's cemetery design book was published in 1843, two years before the cemetery was opened. There is no evidence to indicate that Loudon's guidelines became design specifications for the new cemetery. However, the simplicity and military-like efficiency of a 'Loudonesque' cemetery design was an appropriate response to the urgent need to establish a cemetery that could cope with the high mortality rates among the garrison population.

The earliest known image of the cemetery is a sketch made in 1845, the same year the cemetery was established, by the military surveyor, Lieutenant T. B. Collinson, of the Royal Engineers. Collinson's sketch records the view from a hill above Causeway Bay looking west. Visible in the centre of the sketch is

Happy Valley with the cemetery and newly-built funeral chapel which was annotated as the 'New Grave Yard'.[2] The area that later became the horse racetrack is shown as agricultural land.

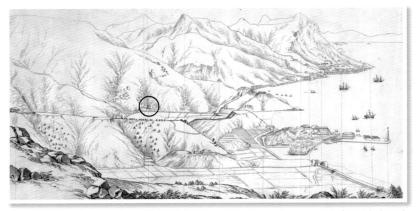

Fig. 3.1   Collinson's 1845 sketch of Hong Kong Island's north coast with funeral chapel circled. Reproduced with the kind permission of the National Archives.

Happy Valley was selected as the site of the new cemetery because it was of sufficient size to accommodate the growing demand for burial space as well as a sufficient distance from the urban area to prevent it being overrun by new development like the first European cemeteries in Wanchai. But there was a third very practical reason for selecting that specific location in Happy Valley — geology.

The landform of Happy Valley can be divided into three basic geological zones.[3] The first is the steep-sided hills that enclose the valley on three sides. The hills are composed of major intrusive igneous rocks, categorised as mainly medium-grained granite. This is a very common rock type in Hong Kong. It is susceptible to weathering and erosion and typically forms steep gradients with relatively thin soil cover. The second geological zone is the broad, flat valley floor (corresponding to the position of the racetrack) which comprises superficial deposits of alluvium, consisting of clay, silt, sand and gravels. The third geological zone is the area occupied by the cemetery gardens on the lower slopes, between the first two zones, comprising superficial debris flow deposits: unsorted sand, gravel, cobbles and boulders.

The influence that these different geological zones have had over time on the settlement pattern and cultural landscape of Happy Valley is significant. Before Hong Kong became a British colony, the fertile flat land of Happy Valley, or Wong Nei Chung (literally: 'yellow mud stream') as it used to be called, supported a number of paddy fields cultivated by the villagers who had settled at the head of the valley. When the British colony was established in 1841 there was little available flat land and the Happy Valley farmland was taken over to establish a camp to help accommodate the garrison. The paddy-field drainage system was destroyed in the process and over time the area became a swampy mosquito breeding ground. Many military personnel who first camped in Happy Valley in the early 1840s died from malarial and other fevers, as recorded on the numerous military memorials in the Hong Kong Cemetery.[4]

In 1846, the fields were cleared and properly drained.[5] Horse-racing started at around this time although the Jockey Club was not established until 1884. The area around the racetrack remained relatively undeveloped until the turn of the century due, in part, to the stigma of the site as a source of fever as well as the relative remoteness of the valley from the main development along the coast. Happy Valley only became popular for residential development as the urban area continued to spread back from the coastline in the early 1900s and a tramline extension was built.[6]

The majority of the Hong Kong Cemetery, St. Michael's Catholic Cemetery and the Parsee Cemetery were established on isolated pockets of alluvial deposits, washed down from the hillside above. The significance of this is that the alluvial soils allow graves to be dug with relative ease compared with the surrounding granite hillside. Furthermore, the sands and gravels that make up the majority of the soil matrix are relatively free-draining, which speeds up the decomposition process.

Selecting this site for the cemeteries was wholly consistent with the expert advice of the day. Loudon's 1843 cemetery design guidelines recommended that, 'the most favourable soil for . . . decomposition is a coarse gravel, subject to be alternately moist and dry'.[7] In contrast, fine grained silts and clays, such as those found on the flat alluvial plain of Happy Valley, formerly cultivated as paddy fields, would have insufficient drainage. In Loudon's words, in the context of London cemeteries, 'in strong clayey soil . . . decomposition does not take place for a very long period.'[8]

From the outset, the cemetery was planned and funded by the colonial government, unlike the privately funded enterprises that established Père Lachaise and Glasgow Necropolis. In the late 1840s, Hong Kong's British garrison outnumbered the Western civilians and the majority of the earliest burials were military personnel and their families. Understandably, this may have influenced the layout of the earliest portions of the cemetery which have the most rigid geometry, typical of military cemeteries where graves are set out in neat rows and columns in areas of lawn.

The proximity of the cemetery to the racetrack can be appreciated in an 1858 sketch showing a race day scene. A small group of cemetery monuments is just visible in the right side of the sketch. The obelisk in the lower left corner, known as 'The Monument', was erected in 1847 by Captain Charles Talbot and officers and crew of the HMS *Vestal* as a memorial to departed shipmates. Public notices announcing funeral ceremonies would state when the processions would pass 'The Monument' en route for the Hong Kong Cemetery. It was the custom for mourners wishing to pay their last respects to gather there to join the entourage.[9]

Fig. 3.2   Sketch of Happy Valley and Racetrack, 1858. Reproduced with the kind permission of the Mary Evans Picture Library/Illustrated London News.

As the city grew and traffic volume increased it was impractical to keep 'The Monument' in the centre of the busy road junction and it was eventually relocated to a site within the cemetery in rather cramped conditions beside other similarly displaced monuments. It is a pity that 'The Monument' was not placed in a more prominent location at, say, a junction of the main path system in the cemetery, befitting its historical landmark status.

Despite the underlying geometry of the cemetery layout, a sketch made in 1866 shows the ground to be rather uneven and some of the headstones and crosses askew, reminiscent of a typical British parish graveyard. To a Westerner, this landscape may have been a poignant reminder of home although not everyone was impressed with the upkeep of the cemetery garden.

In 1865, an article in the *China Mail* expressed the hope that Mr Donaldson, the grounds keeper, could keep the cemetery in order to 'reduce the luxuriant foliage in some places, plant trees and shrubs in others'.[10] At this time, the cemetery did not have a clearly defined style, falling uneasily somewhere between a run-down churchyard and a military cemetery. One reason for the criticism and lack of landscape character may have been that the cemetery had been filling up fast in the twenty years since it opened. By 1865, it is recorded that there were 3,100 graves — almost one-third of the total today.[11] The original caption that accompanied the relatively benign 1866 sketch of the cemetery, reproduced below, is a reminder of the health hazards faced by those living and working in Hong Kong in the early years of the colony.

Fig. 3.3   Sketch of Colonial Cemetery and the Racetrack, 1866
'The races took place last week in the "Happy Valley". Our festivities remind one of the Egyptian banquets over which a skull presided . . . Nearest of all are the graves of the 200 victims of last year's economical arrangements; of those slain by the pestilential miasma of the night, by the deadly vapours of the Kowloon marshes, and by the overpowering rays of a tropical sun dealing death through roofs of matting. The racing week, nevertheless went off as pleasantly as could be expected; but the fatal remembrances of last year threw a shadow over a festival presided over by such ghastly witnesses.' (Reproduced with the kind permission of the Mary Evans Picture Library/Illustrated London News.)

Despite the pressure on the cemetery's resources, a photograph taken around 1890, shows action was taken to improve the overall quality of the planting and general landscape character. It is evident that the vegetation cover has matured, peripheral copses of trees seem denser and there are more ornamental monuments.

Fig. 3.4   Photograph of the Colonial Cemetery and funeral chapel, circa 1890. Reproduced with the kind permission of the Hong Kong Museum of History.

One notable constant feature in illustrations and photos of the cemetery at this time is the attractive cross-shaped funeral chapel at the heart of the site. Built in 1845, it is understood to be the oldest surviving example of colonial architecture in Hong Kong. Careful comparison between archive photographs and the present condition suggests that the chapel has undergone partial reconstruction at some time in the past with an extension to the southern arm of the cross that changed the original + shape to a more typical † cruciform. The extension appears to have functioned as a vestry or store room with independent access door and additional windows on the south gable. It is not visible from inside the chapel. Unfortunately, no record drawings of the original layout of the chapel appear to exist making more detailed comparison impossible. Nevertheless, the heritage significance of the chapel appears finally to have been recognised by the Antiquities and Monuments Office which raised its status from no grading whatsoever to Grade I Historic Building (one step below 'monument') in 2009.

By the 1890s, the Hong Kong Cemetery had taken on a number of 'Loudonesque' features. The level ground around the main entrance and chapel had been laid out in a simple geometric grid. Terraces had been formed on the higher ground and were linked by a simple network of stairs and gently curving footpaths that followed the contours of the hillside. Although not so grand in scale as the large European city cemeteries like Père Lachaise or Glasgow Necropolis, the Hong Kong Cemetery would likely have met with Loudon's approval. It had acquired an easily distinguishable cemetery landscape with tasteful memorials set in a garden-like setting, albeit a relatively plain garden of military bearing.

There are two basic types of memorial in the cemetery: headstones that mark the graves of individuals and monuments that do not mark a grave but commemorate collectively the loss of a group of people, such as members of a ship's crew or military garrison personnel and their families. The earliest examples of each are made from grey granite. Granite is the most common local stone in Hong Kong and it would have been the natural choice for those commissioning and making memorials.

To import more exotic ornamental stone such as marble from overseas would have been time-consuming and very expensive in the mid-1800s. Even quarried and dressed local granite would have been a valuable commodity in the early days of the colony, as suggested by the reported theft of cemetery headstones during the 1850s and 1860s.[12] Before the Hong Kong Cemetery was established in Happy Valley, Europeans were buried in adjoining Protestant and Catholic cemeteries in Wanchai. The site was on an area of hillside between Queen's Road East and Kennedy Road, to the east of today's Pacific Place 3 commercial development. These first cemeteries filled up quickly and were closed once the new, larger cemetery was established in Happy Valley in 1845. Over the next twenty years the Wanchai cemeteries fell into a state of disrepair and it was observed that some of the granite headstones started to disappear only to reappear shortly after for sale to new clients, slightly slimmer and with new inscriptions. By 1889, all remaining headstones in the Wanchai cemeteries had been cleared,[13] forty-eight of them having been moved to the Hong Kong Cemetery in Happy Valley.

Since the graves in the Hong Kong Cemetery are permanent, relatives and friends of the deceased were more likely to invest in a good quality, well-crafted headstone. Like the other nineteenth-century European cemetery gardens, this meant that a high standard of memorial design was established from the outset.

The earliest granite memorial designs are either simple upright tablets or box tombs. The tablets were typically about 15 centimetres thick and stand around 1.5 metres high. They have a simple rectangular shape, sometimes with a slightly peaked top and simple inscription recording the name and dates of birth and death of the deceased. The buried portion of stone that anchors it in place is usually equivalent to about half the height. As a rule of thumb, a 30-centimetre cube of granite would weigh around 80 kilograms. So, before stepping in front of a leaning headstone to read the details of an inscription, it is worth remembering that it may weigh close to a tonne. Obelisks and taller monuments will weigh many times more and should never be rocked to check their stability.

The oldest grave in the cemetery, dated 18 June 1841, belongs to Commander William Brodie, of HM Troopship *Rattlesnake*, whose grave is a very solid-looking granite box tomb. This grave, and several others, predate the opening of the Hong Kong Cemetery in 1845 because, as noted above, they were moved from the Wanchai Cemetery when it closed. Box tombs are made from five or six panels of granite held together with iron pins or clamps and would have been significantly more expensive than the simpler tablet memorials. They fell out of fashion after the 1850s. The box itself is purely ornamental and does not function like a sarcophagus.

Some of the most interesting granite headstones are those with a nautical theme, e.g., anchors and capstans, in remembrance of sailors. Cross designs vary from simple shapes to more complex Celtic crosses with knot patterns. Round or square obelisks are common and a number have intentionally broken tops. This indicates that the person's life was 'cut off' at a young age — the fate of many young sailors and soldiers who were posted here in the mid- to late 1800s. On the other hand, some obelisks are broken because of poor maintenance or natural weathering and ground settlement. It is important to make the distinction and consider repairing the broken ones.

As trade and transport connections with Hong Kong improved, alternative types of stone could be imported at a reasonable cost. White marble became the most popular choice after local granite and by 1900 accounted for about half of new headstones in the cemetery. The more elaborate designs were typically carved overseas and imported to Hong Kong with local stonemasons preparing the plinth, erecting the headstone and perhaps adding the inscription. Customers would select the desired carving from a catalogue or from a stonemason's existing stock.[14]

Marble is a metamorphic rock. It originates as a sedimentary limestone that is converted by intense heat and pressure within the earth's crust into a much denser stone. It has a finer texture than granite and can be carved with more detail. A cost-effective option was to build a large headstone or monument from the cheaper local granite, then inlay a thin slab of marble to display the detailed inscription.

As might be expected, the older sections of the cemetery, closer to the chapel, are recognisable by the larger clusters of heavy granite memorials and the newer sections are located on the more remote upper terraces. However, beyond this simple analysis, the pattern of materials used and sequence of expansion is not clear-cut. For example, in many older sections there has been infill of individual plots, particularly during the 1960s and 1970s, by memorials made from a variety of imported ornamental marbles and coloured granites. In addition, a large number of nineteenth-century granite memorials had to be relocated to available spaces throughout the cemetery to make way for the Aberdeen Tunnel construction in the mid-1970s.

This new fashion in marble headstones introduced an extended family of finely sculpted angels and cherubs into the cemetery. These pristine white figures brightened up the duller tones of the older granite headstones until, that is, late twentieth-century air pollution blackened them. The marble also gave more freedom of expression in headstone design and a whole new vocabulary of icons and symbols was established. Traditional crosses, angels and anchors remained popular but were carved more delicately and supplemented with more naturalistic elements such as birds and flowers. A glossary of the most common icons that can be seen in the cemetery is included in Appendix 1.

Granite tablet   Granite box tomb   Granite bodystone

Granite Celtic cross   Granite anchor/cross   Marble angel

Granite Japanese obelisk   Granite broken column   Timber cross

Fig. 3.5   Selection of different types of memorial

In addition to the type of stone and carved icons, changes in funerary fashion can also be plotted by comparing the wording and tenor of epitaphs. The earliest headstone inscriptions tend to be restricted to terse biblical references in keeping with the stricter moral codes of the Victorian era. Some examples in the cemetery include:

1869
Be thou faithful unto death and I will give thee a crown of life Rev. 2:10
Blessed are the dead which die in the Lord Rev. 14:13

1887
Thy will be done

1890
The Lord gave and the Lord hath taken away
Blessed be the name of the Lord Job 1:21

Some of the most poignant are the monuments that simply list dozens of military personnel and their families who succumbed to the harsh climate of Hong Kong. No names are given and there is no epitaph. The memorial plaque for the 95th Regiment records the following:

Died of fever from June to 30 September 1848
9   *Sergeants*
8   *Corporals*
4   *Drummers*
67   *Privates*
4   *Women*
4   *Children*

By the late 1800s and early 1900s, a few lines of poetry were sometimes used instead of verses of scripture. These epitaphs often reveal more about the individual and how they died. In some, there is also a more upbeat tone that celebrates the person's life as well as mourns their loss. In others, as shown below, the choice of words such as the deceased being laid to 'ripen' or an individual being 'very very gay' may have been perfectly normal and innocent at the time but may make us cringe today.

1895
Rocks and storm I'll fear no more
When on that eternal shore
Drop the anchor: furl the sail
I am sheltered from the gale

1899
A bright light from our ship has gone
A comrade whom we all knew well
At such a time we little thought
Our X'mas chimes should toll the knell
In the midst of joy a life would cease
Tho' gone before may he rest in peace

(Epitaph for a 20-year-old sailor who fell from aloft while helping to decorate his ship on Christmas Eve 1899)

1900
We laid them down to sleep
But not in hopes forlorn
We laid them but to ripen there
Till that great glorious morn

1905
Tread lightly o'er the stranger's grave
He came from o'er the sea
No mother watched his dying bed
No voice said live for me

1916
Her cheery face, her loving smile,
Are pleasant to recall;
She had a kindly word for each,
And died beloved by all.

1947
The light that shone around him in life
Gleams more beautifully in after life

1953
He was young, he was happy
He was very very gay
The world lay open at his feet

Although the details are usually limited to names, dates and places, headstone inscriptions provide a helpful starting point in researching past events. Newspaper archives and official inquest reports can add valuable details since, out of respect, the tragic personal circumstances of, say, deaths by suicide are usually left off the headstone inscriptions. In his study of the garrison graves in the Hong Kong Cemetery, Bard records that, in addition to combat injuries and disease, suicide and accidents were common causes of death among the military personnel stationed in Hong Kong.

Many of the accidents were due to being drunk and disorderly and others were sheer bad luck and carelessness. An example of the latter is the sailor who fell into the harbour when waiting to hire a sampan to return to his ship. His headstone inscription reads that he 'accidentally drowned' whereas evidence presented at the inquest revealed that 'the officer was answering the call of nature when he lost his balance and fell'.[15] Understandably, 'accidentally drowned' makes a more sensitive epitaph than 'fell into the harbour while urinating'.

In Western cemeteries, similar changes in epitaph fashion occurred between the nineteenth and twentieth centuries and it is not uncommon to find humorous epitaphs, some of which may have sinister undertones. The following inscription has appeared in various forms in a number of cemeteries.

> Remember man as you pass by;
> As you are now so once was I,
> As I am now, so you must be,
> Therefore prepare to follow me.

This is not funny at all but underneath someone added:

> To follow you I'm not content
> Until I know which way you went.

The closest to this sentiment recorded in the Hong Kong Cemetery, but without the witty footnote, are two inscriptions that read:

> Young man pause and think
> I'm in eternity and you are on the brink

> Death laid here
> A man good and true
> A prayer please
> It might have been you

The Westerner's taste for strolling through a cemetery looking for amusing or unusual epitaphs must appear to local Hong Kong residents to be morbid or, at best, eccentric. However, in the West, epitaphs are considered to be an opportunity to have the last word, be it a word of wisdom, warning, woe or wit. Epitaphs in the Hong Kong Cemetery do not include much wit, which is perhaps a little surprising given the black humour sometimes (wrongly) associated with the name 'Happy Valley'. However, it may be a consequence of the tragic loss of so many military personnel and their families in the early years of the colony that established a more sombre tone from the outset. Up to one hundred young men died each month from plagues and fevers during the hot humid summer seasons in the 1840s and 1850s. In this context humorous epitaphs would, understandably, have been regarded as insensitive and flippant. Nevertheless, with or without humour, each memorial tells a story not just about the deceased but contributes to the broader social history of Hong Kong.

In parallel with the trend of increasingly decorative memorials, the cemetery planting took on a more lush and exotic appearance. In the latter half of the nineteenth century, the sombre planting style advocated by Loudon was being challenged by British cemetery managers as being too dull and uninspiring.[16] Instead, they wanted to add more seasonal colour and variety of trees and shrubs. From 1890 until around 1910, keeping in step with these trends in the West, the Hong Kong Cemetery completed its comprehensive transformation from a rather bland graveyard to a more ornamental and colourful cemetery garden, thanks to the work of the staff at the Botanical Gardens.

The idea of setting up public botanical gardens was conceived as early as 1848. Government approval was granted in 1856 and the portion of the present garden now known as the 'Old Garden' finally opened in 1864. In 1871 the New Garden was officially added to the Botanical Gardens and Charles Ford was appointed the first superintendent. Ford was a dedicated and energetic botanist and promoted the exchange of seeds, plants and dried specimens between other botanical gardens around the world, including Australia, Japan, Singapore, Trinidad, India, Germany, Taiwan, England and Canton.[17] He also established Hong Kong's extensive herbarium that is currently looked after by the Agriculture, Fisheries and Conservation Department.

Ford is perhaps best known for his initiation of large-scale forestry projects. During the 1870s and 1880s, millions of trees were planted on Hong Kong Island, Kowloon and Lantau, transforming the uplands of the 'barren rock' into the relatively lush woodlands that we often take for granted today. The Botanical and Afforestation Department was also responsible for planting street trees and landscaping Government House and public amenity areas, including the cemetery. Typical entries in the Department's annual reports at this time state:

> Colonial Cemetery — Trees were planted in various places and a good deal of turfing was done. [18]

> Colonial Cemetery
> As usual, a large amount of turfing was done. New shrubs were planted in various places to fill up vacancies caused by some of the older plants dying out. Many trees which had displaced monuments were cut down.[19]

In the same way that the bare Hong Kong hillsides were transformed into woodlands, the department enhanced the previously sparse landscape of the Colonial Cemetery with extensive new planting, introducing exotic tree and shrub species. Ford's successors, notably S. T. Dunn (superintendent from 1903 to 1910) and W. J. Tutcher (superintendent from 1910 to 1920), continued the work of the renamed Botanical and Forestry Department.

A photograph taken around 1910 shows how dramatically the cemetery landscape had been transformed. The mature trees, an ornamental pool and fountain, vine-covered trellises and clipped shrubs in stone pots almost conceal the cemetery headstones and monuments in the background. The first impression is that the scene is somewhere in the Botanical Gardens or a public park rather than a cemetery.

Fig. 3.6   Looking north towards Hong Kong Cemetery fountain, circa 1910. Reproduced with the kind permission of the Hong Kong Museum of History.

The fountain is an important feature in the cemetery as a metaphor for God. The key Bible reference for this is Jeremiah 2:13: 'My people have committed two sins: they have forsaken me, the spring of living water, and have dug their own cisterns, broken cisterns that cannot hold water.' Also, as mentioned in the first chapter, the shape of the fountain is one used in several cultures (including Jewish, Parsee and Islamic design) to represent the flow of life-giving water from the Garden of Eden to the four corners of the earth.

It is unclear exactly when the fountain was built as no records of the blueprint have survived. The fountains in the adjoining Parsee Cemetery and nearby Jewish Cemetery on Shan Kwong Road are similar in design but, once again, accurate records of when these fountains were built no longer exist. One hint at the approximate age of the Hong Kong Cemetery fountain is suggested by its presence in the 1910 photograph and absence from the 1890 photograph, suggesting it was installed sometime in the intervening twenty-year period — perhaps as a centennial project?

The trees in the background of the 1910 fountain photograph also suggest a tenuous horticultural connection to Loudon's preference for conifers in Western cemeteries. The tallest trees visible are Chinese Red Pine (*Pinus massoniana*) — conifers planted extensively by the Botanical and Afforestation Department in their forestry projects. Some remnants of these stands of pine can still be found in peripheral areas of the cemetery today. Strictly speaking, although the canopy of a Chinese Red Pine does not cast a particularly deep shadow, it is not the kind of conifer that Loudon favoured. He preferred slender, cone-shaped trees such as Cypress or Juniper that have a darker, more sombre green colour and cast negligible shadow, ensuring drier conditions around the graves.

However, another photograph of the fountain from a different angle, also dated around 1910, provides a much stronger connection to Loudon's design principles. This second view shows some cone-shaped, semi-mature Norfolk Island Pines (*Araucaria heterophylla*) that are definitely 'Loudonesque' in character. Although not used exclusively throughout the cemetery, these tall, dark green, conical pine trees were planted in sufficient numbers in the lowland area to create a distinctive landscape character, different from other public parks and gardens. Once mature, Norfolk Island Pines tower above broadleaf trees like huge fingers pointing heavenwards. Some of these giants can still be seen in the cemetery today and one of them is included on government's Register of Old and Valuable Trees.

Fig. 3.7 Looking west towards Hong Kong Cemetery fountain, circa 1910, with a good example of a conical Norfolk Island Pine to the right of the path. Reproduced with the kind permission of the Hong Kong Museum of History.

Although the majority of the cemetery's surviving trees are broadleaf species and not 'Loudonesque' conical conifers, they should be regarded as a practical response to the local sub-tropical climate, providing welcome shade to visitors. Rather than detracting from the sombre atmosphere of the site these tropical broadleaf tree species, in combination with the cluster of Norfolk Island Pines, are an appropriate interpretation of an imported cemetery garden philosophy.

The cemetery landscape can be subdivided into three basic types: lowland lawn and shrub areas, stands of mature ornamental trees, and upland secondary woodland. An attractive feature throughout the cemetery is that memorials are all located in grass areas that are frequently mown. In the lowland lawn area this is further enhanced by occasional clumps of flowering shrubs. The most common ornamental shrubs are listed below.

Table 3.1   Most common ornamental shrubs

Botanical Name	Common Name
Duranta repens	Golden Dewdrop
Hibiscus rosa-sinensis	Chinese Hibiscus
Ixora chinensis	Chinese Ixora
Lantana camara	Common Lantana
Ligustrum sinense	Chinese Privet
Thunbergia erecta	Bush Clockvine

Of these shrubs, the Chinese Ixora and Common Lantana are particularly good food sources for a number of butterfly species. While the shrubs in communal areas are pruned regularly, the shrubs within grave plots are (with a few exceptions) typically unkempt and overgrown.

Most of the mature ornamental trees are located in the older and more formal portions of the cemetery, close to the chapel, or on the woodland fringe of the lowland area. Although many of the trees are indigenous, over time numerous exotic species have been introduced. Left to mature for decades in the relatively undisturbed and spacious surroundings of the cemetery, there is now an excellent collection of handsome trees, six of which are on the 'Old and Valuable Tree Register'.[20] Their locations are shown on the tour map in Chapter 4.

Table 3.2   Old and valuable trees in the Hong Kong Cemetery

Tour Stop	Botanical Name	Common Name
3	*Crateva unilocularis*	Spider Tree
6	*Araucaria heterophylla*	Norfolk Island Pine
8	*Cassia siamea*	Kassod Tree
10	*Swietenia mahogani*	West Indies Mahogany
12	*Litchi chinensis*	Lychee
35	*Ficus virens var. sublanceolata*	Big-leaved Fig

Note: only two of these tree species (Lychee and Big-leaved Fig) are commonly regarded as being native to Hong Kong.

The majority of the upper slopes between terraces and along banks of streams, in more remote parts of the cemetery, are well-vegetated by belts of trees, often with a tangled understorey of shrubs and herbs. The slope planting is the result of reinstatement efforts upon completion of the site formation works to build the terraces and access footpaths. The species mix is an interesting blend of typical hillside and streamside forest trees, found throughout Hong Kong, and both indigenous and exotic flowering ornamental trees, planted either singly or in small stands. Appendix 2 shows the list of existing tree species in the cemetery.

In addition to the evolution of memorial and planting design, described above, the Hong Kong Cemetery also exhibits an equally colourful history of cultural diversity. It is commonly understood that the Hong Kong Cemetery was for the exclusive use of European Protestants and that the other cemeteries in Happy Valley would cater for other minority groups such as the Catholic, Muslim, Parsee and Jewish communities. However, in practice it did not work out quite like that. There are numerous memorials to Chinese and Eurasians, e.g., Yeung Kui Wan, a close friend and colleague of Dr Sun Yat Sen, Sir Kai Ho Kai, Sir Robert Ho Tung, Sir Robert's wife and his wife's Chinese servant.

Over time, the Hong Kong Cemetery has accommodated any minority groups that had no cemetery of their own. One such group was Japanese immigrants. There is a large cluster of Japanese graves, 465 in all, on a fairly remote upper terrace. The largest of these is a pristine white obelisk commemorating the Japanese people in general who lived and died in Hong Kong. The inscription can be translated roughly as 'comfort to the bereaved'. There used to be some Japanese graves in a cemetery in So Kon Po but they were all relocated to the Hong Kong Cemetery around 1922.[21]

The rich cultural diversity of Hong Kong can soon be appreciated after a short stroll through the cemetery. Choice of stone colour, shape of headstone, icons and epitaphs, all help distinguish one culture from another. For example, to name a few: sailors' headstones often have anchors; many of the German headstones are made from polished black granite; Russian headstones depict the Orthodox cross with two horizontal bars and one slanted; the Scots often have a Celtic cross; Japanese headstones are typically short square obelisks; military and police headstones are uniform in size and shape and headstones of masons can be spotted by their set square and compasses icon.

The Hong Kong Cemetery and the neighbouring Parsee, Catholic, Muslim and Jewish cemeteries are a microcosm of the diverse nationalities, faiths and cultures that make Hong Kong special. However, one key distinction between the Hong Kong Cemetery and its neighbours is that there is not such a clear-cut cultural identity in the Hong Kong Cemetery. To be buried in the Parsee, Catholic, Muslim or Jewish cemeteries one must belong to that faith — no exceptions.[22]

In addition to the diversity of nationalities, cultures and faiths represented in the Hong Kong Cemetery there are also, upon closer inspection, many colourful stories to tell about the diverse challenges that were faced and met by the brave and enterprising souls who helped establish Hong Kong as a vibrant city. The guided tour in the next chapter tells brief stories associated with a cross-section of the people interred in the cemetery including a Christian missionary, an assassinated political revolutionary, the victim of a tiger attack, a military hero and, of course, successful businessmen.

The end of an era and beginning of decline

Between 1845 and 1910, the cemetery evolved from a simple graveyard into a cemetery garden that reflected the fashion, taste and style of a variety of minority cultures. Arguably, the cemetery looked its best around the period 1910 to 1920. Photographs from this period show a lush and well-tended landscape, a sparkling fountain and bright white marble memorials. On 6 June 1913, the *South China Morning Post* printed an article entitled 'Lest We Forget' that described the Hong Kong Cemetery as:

> an extremely beautiful spot, for all around is to be seen the rugged grandeur of nature's own handiwork; the free elemental play of stream and sky and mountain — a truly wonderful background, and a magnificent object lesson of the infinite and vastness of things.[23]

It is interesting to note the Chinese view of Hong Kong's cemeteries at this time. In 1909, Mr Lau Chu-pak, a leader of the Chinese community and member of the Sanitary Board, quoted Confucius as saying that burial places should not resemble pleasure gardens and should be in harmony with those who weep and mourn.[24]

It is unclear if this was a direct criticism of the Hong Kong Cemetery. After all, the cemetery had, by this time, taken on the appearance of a typical Western cemetery garden. Presumably, the cemetery had managed to avoid the excesses of a 'pleasure garden' and had struck a more harmonious balance for mourners because, two years later, in 1911, the cemetery obviously caught the eye of eighteen leading members of the Chinese community who were seeking to establish their own permanent cemetery. They petitioned the government, writing:

> On behalf of themselves and their fellow countrymen who have made this Colony their home . . . that for the last few years the question of a permanent cemetery has become acute among that section of the Chinese inhabitants which has resided in Hong Kong for a large number of years and has no intention of returning to China save for temporary purposes — social, commercial or otherwise.[25]

This, for the first time, broke with the Chinese tradition of sending the remains of the deceased back to the Mainland to be buried in the town or village of their birth. These leading members of the Chinese community wanted Hong Kong and not Mainland China to be their final resting place. The petition stated that the cemeteries available to non-Christian Chinese were not permanent and, furthermore, that:

> Not one of the said cemeteries is well laid out and planted with shrubs, trees, ornamental plants and flowers [and] that the Colonial Cemetery otherwise known as the Protestant Cemetery is nicely laid out and kept.[26]

The petition was granted and in 1913 a plot of land was allocated for the Chinese Permanent Cemetery in Aberdeen. The Hong Kong Cemetery had by now completed its transition from a simple graveyard that had 'dampened the spirits' of nineteenth-century race-goers to an attractive cemetery garden that had become a role model for local cemetery garden design.

Unfortunately, not long after this accolade the Hong Kong Cemetery began a slow but steady decline that continued for the remainder of the twentieth century. Today, the cemetery looks deceptively neat and tidy to the casual visitor or passer-by. However, on closer inspection it soon becomes obvious that all is not well. Many of the memorials are dilapidated. Some have toppled over, their broken pieces lying face down in the grass. Others lean precariously, defying gravity. Inscriptions have faded, white marble carvings are now blackened by the effects of pollution and the once proud fountain is dry and filled with soil and shrubs.

This is surprising when compared with the well-maintained headstones in the neighbouring Muslim, Catholic, Parsee and Jewish Cemeteries. A cemetery garden is supposed to be a place to see tasteful memorials in an attractively landscaped setting, and yet, for decades, scant attention has been paid to protecting the Hong Kong Cemetery's irreplaceable ten thousand or so granite and marble memorials recording 165 years of Hong Kong's history.

Reasons for decline

Similar problems of cemetery decline in the early to mid-1900s occurred in Europe. The private ventures and joint stock companies that established the cemetery gardens were going bankrupt because the cemeteries had largely filled up. The lots had been sold as permanent graves and once the space ran out there was little or no revenue being generated for their upkeep. In the majority of cases, responsibility for maintaining the cemeteries was passed to the local authority who, understandably, adopted a low-key maintenance regime to minimise costs to the taxpayer.

By contrast, the Hong Kong Cemetery was not a privately funded venture. The government paid for its establishment and has been funding the cemetery's maintenance ever since from tax payers' money. What made a difference in the early years was the enthusiastic and pro-active enhancement of the cemetery landscape by the Botanical Garden staff in the late 1800s and early 1900s coinciding with the timing and spirit of the European cemetery garden movement. This fortuitous blip on the graph does not seem to have been sustained and the condition of the cemetery went into a gradual but steady decline during the last century — not due to any one event, but as a result of several factors, including an identity crisis, the ravages of war and road building, natural deterioration and human error.

The period from 1910 to 1920 is suggested as an arbitrary 'watershed' of the cemetery's change in fortune as it was a period of very public and emotional debate about the status of the cemetery. In 1903, the Public Health and Buildings Ordinance had allocated exclusive areas in the cemetery for burial of military officers, civil servants, residents for over twenty-one years, residents for over seven years, children and destitutes.[27] It is quite common for cemeteries to allocate portions for a particular culture group. Nevertheless, there were other lingering complaints about conditions in the cemetery that the 1903 Ordinance did not resolve satisfactorily.

Two major complaints that sparked heated debate were the burning of joss sticks and setting off firecrackers within the cemetery at non-Christian graves and a general lack of sites in Hong Kong for burial of wealthy Chinese members of the community. The joss stick and firecracker problem occurred mainly when relatives paid their respects at the Buddhist Japanese graves and had given offence to visitors to nearby Christian graves.[28] The 1909 Christian Cemetery Ordinance sought to resolve this issue by identifying portions of the cemetery that would be dedicated and consecrated for Christian burials with a separate area for non-Christian burials. It is interesting to note that today the portion of the cemetery designated for Japanese graves is one of the best maintained, thanks largely to organised grave sweeping visits by Japanese high school students each spring, since 2000, as part of their heritage education.

The second major issue of finding equivalent burial sites to satisfy the demand from the wealthy members of the Chinese community proved more difficult to resolve. Sites had been allocated for Chinese burials in various locations around Hong Kong but they tended to be areas of bare hillside where the government retained the right to resume the land and order remains to be exhumed and buried elsewhere. In the absence of auspicious sites for a permanent Chinese cemetery that could accommodate the larger traditional 'armchair–shaped' graves, members of the wealthier Chinese community started making requests for burial lots in the Hong Kong Cemetery.

The case for equal rights to be buried in the Hong Kong Cemetery was made eloquently by Mr Lau Chu-pak — a member of the Sanitary Board and co-owner of the *Hong Kong Telegraph*. In both committee meetings and newspaper editorials during 1909 Mr Lau did not pull his punches. Here are two quotes from Mr Lau referring to the sub-standard sites previously proposed for a Chinese cemetery and the public status of the Hong Kong Cemetery.

> Fancy the outcry there would be among the elite if the remains of the deceased of their predecessors were subject to removal at the whim and caprice of some insignificant official in a Government Department. That in itself should constitute a plea for the Chinese that they have a right of interment in the Colonial Cemetery.

> The Colonial or Protestant — or whatever fancy name anybody might wish to call it — the public cemetery of Hong Kong is maintained out of the rates and taxes provided by the residents in the Colony. It is no more a private institution than the public gardens. No sect or body has a right to say that it has any particular claim on the domain, as far as we can make out, all have an equal right to interment.[29]

It is not hard to imagine that such a sustained criticism of the unfair allocation of cemetery space from within and outside the 'system' put considerable heat under the bureaucracy of the day and helped expedite a solution, i.e., an area in the cemetery set aside for non-Christian burials (1910) and a plot of land in Aberdeen set aside for establishment of the first Permanent Chinese Cemetery (1913).

This aspect of cultural identity has proved to be an important influence on the declining condition of the Hong Kong Cemetery in the following years. The Muslim, Catholic, Parsee and Jewish cemeteries in Happy Valley are in much better condition. In these cemeteries, interments are strictly limited to those who professed the respective faith and each cemetery manager takes a pride in ensuring the cemeteries are well maintained with no leaning or fallen memorials. If the Hong Kong Cemetery really had been a cemetery restricted to Protestant burials under, say, the auspices of the Anglican Church instead of a government department, then there would surely have been a stronger sense of identity, ownership and motivation to maintain the site better.

When first established, the Hong Kong Cemetery was placed under the charge of the Colonial Chaplain, who kept a record of burials while the government covered the maintenance costs. However, this early link to the Anglican community was eroded when the cemetery was placed under the jurisdiction of the Sanitary Board[30] — a government body created in 1883 and a precursor to the former Urban Council and current Food and Environmental Hygiene Department.

A revealing postscript to the 1909 brouhaha on the right of Chinese to be buried in the Hong Kong Cemetery is an exchange of correspondence between the Colonial Secretariat and dean of St. John's Cathedral on 28 October 1954. Mr R. J. C. Howes of the Colonial Secretariat responded to the dean's query regarding the official stance on eligibility for burial at the cemetery:

> There is no Cemetery Ordinance nor are there any Government Regulations but the standing instructions under which the Urban Services Department operate over this matter, which date from pre-war, are that:
>
> 1. No persons of Chinese race are allowed to be buried in the Colonial Cemetery.
> 2. Eurasians may not be buried in the Colonial Cemetery unless;
>   (a) they have a European surname
>   (b) they are Christians
>   (c) that special permission is given by the Cemeteries Select Committee or in an emergency by the Chairman, Urban Council or the Secretary.[31]

The Colonial Secretariat further stressed that scarcity of space in the cemetery meant that permission was reserved for those who have no other burial sites provided elsewhere.

War also took its toll on the cemetery. During World War II, under Japanese occupation, the majority of Hong Kong's hillside woodland and urban trees were felled for fuel and raw materials for building. The Hong Kong Cemetery was no exception. A photograph taken by Hedda Morrison in 1946, a year after Japan's surrender, shows the extent of vegetation loss in the cemetery with only small pockets of woodland remaining.

Fig. 3.8   View over Happy Valley cemeteries towards the racetrack and Victoria Harbour, 1946. Reproduced with the kind permission of the Harvard-Yenching Library.

Some of the headstones suffered what appears to be war damage from shrapnel while others were stripped of their lead lettering. During wartime all basic necessities were in desperately short supply and it is understandable that valuable raw materials such as lead would be scavenged and bartered.

After the war further large-scale afforestation was carried out throughout Hong Kong, particularly in association with water catchment areas to prevent soil erosion and in urban areas to stabilise slopes. In 1953, the Urban Services Department took over the management responsibility of public cemeteries. Subsequent aerial photographs in the 1960s show the post-war tree planting establishing well on slopes within and adjacent to the cemetery.

Ironically, in 1974, having endured over a century of damage from typhoons and the ravages of war, the most devastating blow to the cemetery's landscape was delivered by Hong Kong's own transport planners and highway engineers when a portion of the cemetery was resumed to accommodate the elevated approach roads and tunnel portals of the Aberdeen Tunnel. A large swathe of lawn and woodland was lost and many historic memorials and monuments had to be relocated within the cemetery or to other cemeteries. If Loudon would have frowned at the addition of ornamental planting, he would surely have turned in his grave at the sight of these ugly concrete flyovers and noisy intrusion of traffic into the heart of Hong Kong's oldest cemetery garden.

In 1991, Dr Solomon Bard completed a report for the Antiquities and Monuments Office on the military graves and monuments in the Hong Kong Cemetery. These are the graves of military personnel who died while serving in Hong Kong and Bard's report gives valuable insight into both the social history of the garrison as well as the physical condition of the cemetery at that time. The report makes several recommendations, two of which relate to protection of the headstones and the adverse impacts of nature and bad maintenance:

> Many graves and monuments, military and civilian, in the peripheral sections of the Cemetery, are in a bad state of neglect. They should be repaired, cleared of vegetation, moss, or lichen, and maintained in good order . . .

> Previous attempts to outline inscriptions on the memorials in black paint, by the Cemetery staff, resulted in many errors. The inscriptions should NOT be outlined in black or any other paint, but should be left alone.[32]

At the same time as Bard was carrying out his report, the government decided that there should be no more permanent burials in Hong Kong due to a lack of available cemetery space. Instead, all new graves would be recycled after seven years, with possible extension to ten years. That is, to make way for new burials, after the seven to ten-year period has expired, the remains would be exhumed, cremated or placed in bone pots and re-interred in columbarium niches. This is not a new concept or practice but the implication is that the timeline of headstone-recorded history and memorial design as an art form has now come to an end. If a grave is no longer permanent, then there is little incentive for the relatives of the deceased to commission a beautiful headstone that will be scrapped seven years later. The intact timeline recorded in the Hong Kong Cemetery headstones from 1845 to 1990 suddenly seems all the more valuable and vulnerable.

Over the last 165 years the memorials have deteriorated due to the effects of weathering, soil subsidence, chemical reactions of different types of stone with pollutants in the air, rusting metalwork, expanding tree roots and bird droppings. As a result, inscriptions have become indistinct and in many cases the headstones have fallen over and broken or are leaning precariously. These natural processes are inevitable but in some cases they have been exacerbated by human error in the choice of material and memorial design as well as botched repairs and neglect.

Since 2000, the Food and Environmental Hygiene Department (FEHD) has been responsible for the day-to-day management of the cemetery, taking care of the grass cutting, path sweeping and generally maintaining the status quo. Depressingly, FEHD is neither in a position to enhance the diversity of the plant species as the Botanical Garden staff did in the late 1800s and early 1900s, nor equipped to prepare a heritage conservation plan for the cemetery and implement a programme of repairs for the broken and deteriorating memorials.[33]

A silver lining to the cloud

Although many of the built heritage resources (memorials) of the cemetery have been allowed to deteriorate badly, the natural heritage resources (flora and fauna) appear to have fared better, thanks in part to the 'hands-off' management approach adopted for the last few decades. It is not possible to make precise comparisons between the plants and animals present today and those present in the cemetery during the late 1800s and early 1900s. The archive data just do not exist. However, there is a way to make general 'then and now' comparisons of biodiversity with the help of the humble butterfly and moth.

During preparation of a plant database for the cemetery in 2004, the author was advised by Dr Gary Ades and Dr Roger Kendrick of Kadoorie Farm Botanical Garden that a simple and reliable way to establish the biodiversity of a site is to study the butterfly and moth populations present. Butterflies and moths are considered by ecologists to be 'umbrella taxa', and widely used as indicators for the assessment of overall biodiversity and evaluation of environmental disturbance. In 1907, J. C. Kershaw, an eminent lepidopterist, wrote in his book, *Butterflies of Hong Kong and South-East China* that 'they [butterflies] stand at the head, not only of all insects, but of the whole organic world, as registers of subtle and elusive change'.[34]

The majority of moths and butterflies are nectarivores, feeding on the nectar of particular flower species. Some moths feed on lichen, such as that found on cemetery headstones. So, if many different varieties of moths and butterflies are discovered in a study area, it follows there must be a wide variety of plant species present to support them.

Fortunately, for the purposes of comparison, there are published studies of butterflies in Hong Kong in the 1890s. An account of butterflies recorded during the winter and spring months of 1892 and 1893 by J .J. Walker (Chief Engineer of the survey ship HMS *Penguin*), highlights the ecological value of the cemeteries in particular. Walker writes:

> By far the most productive locality for butterflies in the island is the Wong-nei-chong, or 'Happy Valley'. . . On all sides except the north, where it is open to the harbour, it is shut in by wooded hills, and on its west side are the European cemeteries, the English one in particular being celebrated for the beauty of the gardens attached to it.[35]

This opinion is supported by observations by the naturalist Sydney B. J. Skertchly, who wrote in 1893 that 'the Happy Valley is the butterflies' paradise'.[36] Why this should be the case is almost certainly due to the introduction of so many exotic plant species by the Botanical Garden staff. Without this intervention in the landscape, Happy Valley would likely have had a normal cross-section of local plant material and would not have been singled out by the lepidopterists as a special site for butterflies.

So, what is the situation today? With the kind help of Dr Roger Kendrick and fellow members of the Hong Kong Lepidopterist Society, butterfly and moth surveys were carried out on 1 October 2004. The butterfly experts walked through the entire cemetery during the afternoon and, by simple observation, were able to count nineteen different butterfly species. At dusk the same day, Dr Kendrick's moth team set up two light box traps on the footpath beside the main stream course and monitored the moth visitors for a three-hour period. The traps comprised a rigid container with a slotted clear plastic cover. Inside was a strong light to lure the moths surrounded by layers of egg-box cardboard. Once moths slip through the slots into the box, they settle calmly on the cardboard layers and are easy to study at close range. Once identified and counted, the light was switched off and the moths released unharmed. A total of twenty-eight different moth species were identified and are listed with the butterflies in Appendix 3.

To carry out a comprehensive butterfly and moth survey, eight to ten visits would normally be required throughout the year to identify species in different seasons. Nevertheless, nineteen butterfly species and twenty-eight moth species on a short survey, on one day, was a good result and suggested that the cemetery may support many times this number (perhaps as many as sixty to eighty species) throughout the year. Indeed, this one-day survey compares very favourably with the Leisure and Cultural Services Department's data on butterfly species recorded in the urban parks throughout Hong Kong, Kowloon and the New Territories. These parks are predominantly ornamental in nature and include a large variety of plant species.

Table 3.3   Butterflies recorded in urban parks

Urban Park	Number of butterfly species recorded
Hong Kong Zoological and Botanical Gardens	19
Hong Kong Park	21
Kowloon Park	22
Tai Po Waterfront Park	17
Tuen Mun Park	16
Yuen Long Park	19

Source: LCSD, *Butterfly Watching in Urban Parks*

Of particular interest is that three of the nineteen butterfly species identified in the survey are considered by the HKLS surveyors to be 'quite rare' and 'unexpected finds in the cemetery'. Furthermore, two of the twenty-eight different moth species are 'likely to be undescribed by science.' Both of these moth species are classified as 'rare', i.e., only two to four previous records and likely restricted to three or less sites in Hong Kong.[37]

Based on the internationally acknowledged use of butterflies and moths as biodiversity indicators, it would seem that the introduction of so many exotic plant species in the cemetery has enriched the overall flora and fauna biodiversity of the site. This provides some very useful guidance for maintaining and further enhancing the natural heritage resources of the cemetery in the future.

Invitation

The foregoing description of the rise and fall of the Hong Kong Cemetery has only managed to scratch the surface of this complex and valuable cultural landscape. To add more flesh to these bones, the reader is now invited to set aside half a day to visit the cemetery and take the self-guided tour in Chapter 4 to experience this heritage site as intended by the nineteenth-century European cemetery garden designers.

The tour should appeal to anyone interested in landscape design, ecology, social history, traditional crafts, and built heritage conservation. It also elaborates on some of the more technical problems arising from natural weathering and human error that contribute to the current condition of the memorials and are in most need of remedial treatment.

4 Self-guided Tour

Churchyards and cemeteries are scenes not only calculated to improve the morals and the taste, and by their botanical riches to cultivate the intellect, but they serve as historical records.

John Claudius Loudon [1]

Tips for the tour

The tour of the Hong Kong Cemetery has been designed as two loops. The lowland loop is suitable for wheelchair access and can be comfortably done in about one hour. The extended tour includes the upland loop which has a number of staircases and steep sections of path. The extended tour, taken at an easy pace, would take around three hours to complete. Before starting the tour there are some common-sense safety and courtesy tips that should be remembered:

- **Wear** comfortable shoes with good grip as some of the paths in the upland loop in shady spots may be slippery when wet.

- **Stay** well back from the edges of platforms as not all of them are guarded by safety handrails.

- **Never** test the stability of a headstone by pushing it and do not stand in front of or lean against a tilted memorial.

- **Be** watchful for other visitors who may be paying their respects by a graveside and talk and walk quietly in order not to disturb them.

The cemetery is divided into many different sections which are identified by small stone blocks beside the footpath. However, the section markers are sometimes difficult to locate and much time can be wasted searching for them. Until better markers are provided, and to avoid confusion with the tour stop numbering, section numbers have been omitted from the guide maps. Instead, the guide maps are drawn to scale with the suggested route clearly marked. Used in combination with the photographs of the points of interest the visitor should be able to avoid any wrong turns.

The cemetery is open every day from 7 a.m. to 7 p.m. between 1 April and 30 September and from 7 a.m. to 6 p.m. between 1 October and 31 March. There are two pedestrian entrances: the main one from Wong Nei Chung Road and a secondary one from Stubbs Road. Both these entrances have steps. For wheelchair access, use the vehicle entrance beside the Cemetery Office on Wong Nei Chung Road but note that this is only open Monday to Friday 9 a.m. to 5 p.m., Saturday from 9 a.m. to noon, and is closed on Sundays and public holidays.

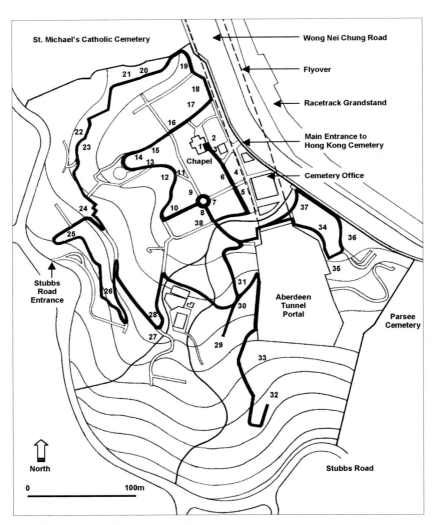

Hong Kong Cemetery Overview Guide Map

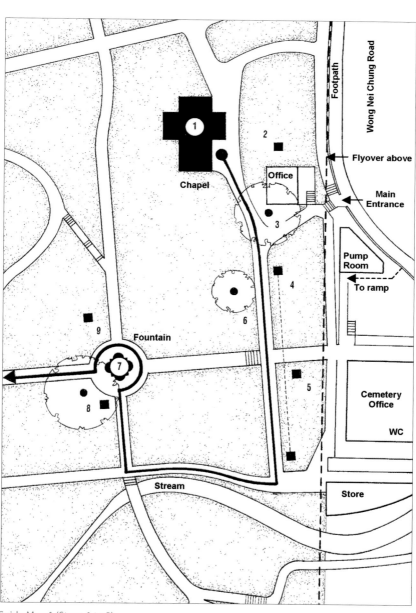

Guide Map 1 (Stops 1 to 9)

Stop 1: **Funeral chapel**

The funeral chapel is believed to be the oldest surviving colonial building in Hong Kong and was designated a Grade I Historic Building in 2009. Built in 1845, the year the cemetery opened, the chapel accommodated funeral services prior to burials. The pointed arch windows are Victorian Gothic in style. Although no record drawings can be traced, careful comparison between archive photographs suggests that the chapel has undergone partial reconstruction. An extension to the southern arm of the cross changed the original + shape to a more typical † cruciform. The extension appears to have functioned as a vestry or store room with an independent access door and additional windows on the south gable. The timber and tiled roof would have been replaced a number of times over the years and was recently repaired under the supervision of the Architectural Services Department.

The chapel is surrounded by some of the cemetery's oldest graves including ornately carved marble and granite memorials. The marble headstones used to be pristine white. Today, at first glance, it may be hard to tell the two materials apart because most of the marble has become blackened by a combination of bacterial and chemical action. Cyanobacteria are the first microbes to colonise new headstones because they only need light and inorganic material to grow. They fix atmospheric nitrogen and provide carbon compounds on the stone surface that can then be used as nutrients by other organisms. However, the major source of discolouration appears to come from air pollution. An excess of sulphur dioxide and nitrogen dioxide emitted from vehicle exhausts and factories causes rain to become acidic. Prolonged exposure to this 'acid rain' converts the surface of marble into gypsum. The gypsum, when combined with carbon particulates, coats the stone in a harmful black crust. Eventually, this unstable crust will crumble away taking with it the headstone inscriptions and detailed carving. It can be cleaned but is a delicate job for experts and, of course, will blacken again without regular maintenance.

Stop2: Karl Gutzlaff

Gutzlaff (1803–51) was a German Lutheran missionary who is best known for his books about China and for being the first Protestant missionary in Bangkok. He took part as a translator in the negotiations during the Opium War (1840–42) and established a training school for Chinese missionaries to work in China. This was an innovative approach to evangelism at that time because China's interior was closed to foreigners. Unfortunately, many of the young 'converts' who were recruited as missionaries were opium addicts and took advantage of Gutzlaff by selling the Christian literature back to the publisher who then sold it again to Gutzlaff. They also used mission trips to trade opium instead of spreading the gospel. Although this scandal brought disgrace to Gutzlaff, who died soon after it was exposed, his missionary school continued and helped send famous missionaries, such as Hudson Taylor, into China. Gutzlaff was a controversial figure but nevertheless illustrates the adventurous spirit of the early years of colonial Hong Kong. His memorial is made from grey granite in the form of a raised box tomb with inlaid white marble plaques.

Stop3: Spider tree (*Crateva unilocularis*)

Gutzlaff's memorial is shaded by some mature trees including a venerable Crateva (*Crateva unilocularis*, commonly known as the Spider tree or Gold-and-Silver tree). This is the first of six trees in the cemetery recorded in the government's 'Old and Valuable Tree Register'. It has a superb show of creamy flowers in late spring and early summer and has been used as a roadside tree throughout Hong Kong. The common names are derived from the long filaments at the centre of the flowers that resemble spiders' legs and the petals which are white at first then gradually turn yellow. Other less welcome trees are the small Chinese banyan seedlings that can often be seen taking root in the joints of memorial stonework. Birds eat the banyan figs but cannot digest the hard seeds at the centre. When the birds pass out the seeds they often land on the memorials in cracks and joints between stone blocks. Boosted by a starter package of fertiliser, courtesy of the birds, the seedlings' vigorous roots will grow rapidly and in a few years can prise apart stonework and crack plaques. If left unchecked they can cause considerable damage to memorials.

Stop 4: **Early military memorials**

Taking the path to the south leads to a row of early granite military memorials. The first group includes two memorials in the form of a broken column symbolising that the deceased died young. Usually only the lower half of the column is installed but in one case the top portion has also been set deliberately onto the plinth. Unlike a number of other columns that have fallen and broken into pieces in other parts of the cemetery, this particular one does not need mending. Other designs include an unusually chunky cross and, at the far end of the row, an interesting castle tower that resembles a 'rook' chess piece. Use of castles in memorial design symbolises strength and protection for the deceased. The cemetery used to extend further downhill from this point towards the tramline but many memorials were relocated to accommodate construction of the Aberdeen Tunnel and highway flyover in the 1970s.

Stop 5: Daniel Richard Caldwell ('Protector of the Chinese')

In the middle of the row of early military memorials is a distinctive and ornately carved column surrounded by iron railings. The memorial is constructed in granite and marble, in memory of an equally colourful character, Daniel R. Caldwell (1816–75). Born in St Helena, Caldwell moved as a child with his family to Penang and then Singapore. As a young man he eventually came to the South China Coast where he worked on opium smuggling ships. He spoke Malay, Hindustani and Portuguese and was able to blend in with the smugglers and pirates, refining his Cantonese and other Chinese dialects in the process. This background proved to be both a blessing and a curse when he later joined the Hong Kong government as a court interpreter and head of detectives accompanying Royal Navy raids against pirates. His linguistic skills and inside knowledge of local piracy proved invaluable to the government but, at times, also put him under suspicion of collusion with his former smuggling associates. One of his government posts was Registrar General and Protector of the Chinese. The title 'Protector of the Chinese' is the one with which Caldwell's life is most closely associated. He continued to play this role to the end of his life, even when no longer a civil servant, by being an informal counsellor to the Chinese community who held him in very high regard. Caldwell's monument is decorated with a variety of masonic symbols and text. Similar symbols can be seen on many other memorials throughout the cemetery, particularly on the headstones of policemen.

Stop 6: Norfolk Island Pine (*Araucaria heterophylla*)

The very tall slender tree on the opposite side of the path from Caldwell's memorial is a Norfolk Island Pine (*Araucaria heterophylla*) — the second of the cemetery's 'Old and Valuable Trees'. Archive photographs from around 1910 record that many more Norfolk Island Pines were planted in this portion of the cemetery. Sadly, only a few have survived the damage inflicted by countless typhoons, wartime felling and highway engineers. The presence of the Norfolk Island Pine is very significant because it suggests that botanical staff responsible for the early cemetery planting applied some of the Western design principles advocated by the highly influential nineteenth-century Scots cemetery designer John C. Loudon. Loudon favoured the use of slender pine trees in cemeteries for practical and aesthetic reasons. Slender pines take up less space, cast less shadow and encourage drier ground conditions. Being evergreen, they shed few needles and minimise maintenance work. Their simple, sombre appearance was considered to be the most appropriate for a cemetery garden and, if planted in sufficient quantities, helped create a cemetery landscape that was distinct from other kinds of public open spaces. In Loudon's day, the pines would have been pruned regularly to keep them in good shape and in scale with their surroundings. Although the Norfolk Island Pines in the Hong Kong Cemetery are now few in number and have been allowed to grow unchecked, it is still possible to imagine the associations they once must have had for cemetery visitors — perhaps symbolising fingers pointing heavenwards or, in the context of the adjacent military memorials, a line of well-drilled soldiers.

Stop 7: **Ornamental fountain**

In the early 1900s the fountain was a focal point in the cemetery. There used to be another ornamental pond at a nearby path junction but it has long since been removed. Sadly, today's view of the fountain sums up how much the cemetery has deteriorated overall in the intervening century. The original stone and cast iron work are still in place. However, the basin is filled in with cement to prevent mosquitoes breeding in puddles of rainwater and the stone pool is now a planter with scruffy shrubs. No longer is the fountain a symbol of God as the spring of living water. The only heavenly reference is an incongruous white marble cherub who has taken up residence where the fountain nozzle used to be and looks suspiciously like a misplaced headstone decoration.

The outline of the pool comprises a central square with semi-circular bays on each side. This pattern is a cross-cultural motif, commonly seen in Islamic art and architecture around the world, as well as closer to home in similar fountains in Happy Valley's Parsee and Jewish Cemeteries. As mentioned in Chapter 1, in the Bible the book of Genesis describes a river watering the Garden of Eden that divided into four headstreams. The four-sided pool is intended to represent these life-giving rivers flowing out of the Garden of Eden to the four corners of the world. Since the original image described in Genesis pre-dates divisions between the Islamic and Christian faiths it is common to both. It is hoped that the fountain could one day be restored to its former glory, minus the cherub.

Stop 8: Tallest monument and Kassod tree (*Cassia siamea*)

Beside the ornamental fountain is the third 'Old and Valuable Tree' — a large Kassod tree (*Cassia siamea*) that produces a generous show of yellow flowers in late summer. This species is native to India and Malaysia and was introduced to Hong Kong in the late 1800s. The monument under the canopy of the Kassod is the tallest in the cemetery and commemorates the large numbers of military personnel of the 59th Regiment and their families (36 women and 107 children) who died from outbreaks of disease in the early years of colonial Hong Kong from 1849 to 1858. Monuments like these do not mark burial sites but are constructed as memorials to an individual or groups of people such as a garrison regiment or ship's crew. An early photo of this monument shows it was originally located beside the memorials at Stop 4 before the intrusion of the highway in the 1970s.

Stop 9: Commander William Brodie

Near the fountain is a cluster of granite box tombs and large tablet headstones. The box tomb belonging to Commander William Brodie of HMS *Rattlesnake* (died 1841, aged 56 years) appears to be the earliest dated grave in the cemetery. Box tombs were expensive memorials that required a lot of stone and soon fell out of fashion. The box itself is empty, the remains being buried in the normal way. The individual panels of stone are normally held together with iron brackets. In time, ground settlement and rusting of the brackets can destabilise the box tombs and there are plenty of crooked examples around the cemetery. Fortunately, the inscriptions carved onto the top of Brodie's box tomb are still legible. Often inscriptions on horizontal surfaces will deteriorate faster because they collect rainwater — a problem that is more serious in colder climates, such as North America or Europe, when ice forms in the grooves of the inscription. The pressure of the ice expanding can then crack and break off small pieces of the carved details.

Apart from being the oldest grave, Brodie's memorial appears to have been one of the most mobile. Naval surgeon, Edward Cree, recorded Brodie's funeral procession with a watercolour sketch and a journal entry dated 18 June 1841, 'Poor old Brodie was buried in the afternoon in the new cemetery in "Happy Valley".' Since the Hong Kong Cemetery was not opened until 1845, where did they bury Brodie?

Cree's account of Brodie's funeral raises two interesting points. Firstly, it confirms that 'Happy Valley' was a common euphemism for a cemetery and has nothing to do with the advent of horse-racing several years later. Secondly, since the government officially designated a plot of land for the colony's first Western burials in Wanchai on 30 August 1841 (two months after Brodie's funeral), it follows that the temporary garrison camp, established the same year in Happy Valley, likely included its own cemetery for military burials before this date. This 'garrison cemetery' would have been a practical measure to cope with the numerous recorded deaths due to the bad sanitation and mosquito problems that plagued Happy Valley during the rainy season. Understandably, the garrison abandoned this camp and it appears that Brodie's grave was relocated to the new Wanchai Cemetery soon after. There, Brodie's remains rested in relative peace, until 1889 when government records show the Wanchai Cemetery was cleared for redevelopment and Brodie's grave returned to Happy Valley, being laid to rest, hopefully for the last time, in the Hong Kong Cemetery.

Cree's watercolour of Happy Valley recording Brodie's funeral procession, 18 June 1841.[2] Reproduced with the kind permission of Dutton, a division of Penguin Group (USA) Inc. and Webb and Bower Publishers Ltd.

Brodie's last command, HMS *Rattlesnake*, was later converted into a survey ship and on 16 October 1849 made the famous rescue of Barbara Crawford Thompson, a Scots girl, who had been shipwrecked in the Torres Strait off the north coast of Australia when she was sixteen years old. Thompson had survived as a captive of the local Kaurareg people for almost five years, despite their reputation for being cannibals.

Please note that Guide Map 2 indicates an alternative ramped path to the next stop that avoids a short flight of steps.

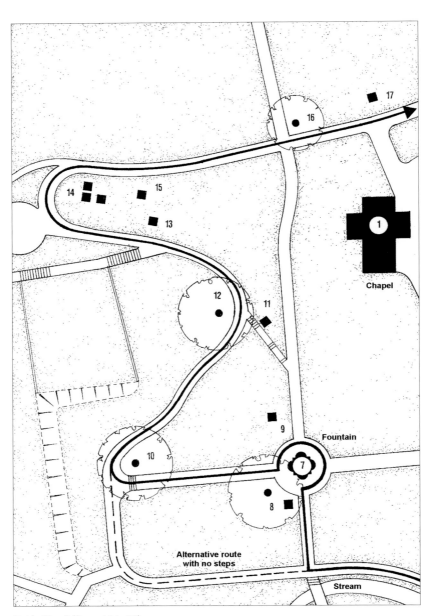

Guide Map 2 (Stops 10 to 17)

Stop 10: **Mahogany tree (*Swietenia mahogani*)**

The Mahogany tree is arguably the best example of this species in Hong Kong. Introduced to Hong Kong from the West Indies, its timber is very hard and favoured for high quality furniture making. Both the Mahogany and the nearby Kassod tree can be seen in photos of the cemetery taken at the end of World War II. Many trees were felled for firewood and building materials during the Japanese occupation and it is most fortunate that the Mahogany survived to become the fourth 'Old and Valuable Tree' in the cemetery.

Magnificent though this tree is, the impact of its roots on nearby memorials is clearly evident. By rule of thumb, a tree's roots generally spread as wide as its canopy and any memorial within its shadow is therefore vulnerable to damage. This dilemma highlights the need to establish a co-ordinated management plan for the cemetery that considers both the built and natural heritage resources together. A lasting solution will likely involve selective pruning of the tree's roots and canopy and resetting dislodged or unstable memorials.

Although the six 'Old and Valuable' trees are clearly labelled, there are many other interesting indigenous and exotic species to be seen in the cemetery. Additional labelling of the different trees would be relatively easy to do and would be in keeping with the traditional multifunctional role of the nineteenth-century cemetery as memorial garden, public park and arboretum.

Stop 11: Tilted tablet memorial

Follow the curved path past the bamboo and stop at the junction with the narrow stepped path on the right. Halfway down the path is a good example of a tablet memorial with a serious tilt. Do not stand in front of it as it weighs around a tonne and is clearly unstable. It is normal for headstones to lean over time and although they may look quaint and add character to the cemetery, they do pose a hazard. Apart from the danger of them toppling over and injuring a visitor to the cemetery, in falling, they can also break and damage the historic inscriptions. To stabilise this headstone would be a simple operation. In this case, the stone would be propped securely and a wedge of soil and turf carefully excavated from the uphill side down to the base of the stone (usually about one-third of the stone's overall height would be underground). The stone would then be gently eased upright and the excavated soil replaced and compacted firmly in the downhill side before finally returfing.

Unfortunately, even this kind of simple preventive measure is not undertaken by the cemetery management. The upkeep and repair of headstones is considered to be the responsibility of the private owners. This policy has had a serious impact on the overall condition of the cemetery and the merits of a different approach are discussed in more detail in the final chapter.

Stop 12: **Lychee tree (_Litchi chinensis_) and bird viewpoint**

On the other side of the path is a magnificent Lychee tree (the fifth 'Old and Valuable Tree' in the cemetery). The nearby bench is a good vantage point from which to view the chapel in its original landscaped setting, which is unusual for a heritage building in urban Hong Kong. If you sit quietly for a few minutes, you will start to notice the birdsong. Some of the most common birds in this portion of the cemetery are sparrows, spotted doves, bulbuls, magpie robins, and cockatoos.

The magpie robin has the sweetest song and is easily identified by its smart black and white markings. When alarmed they make a hissing sound and flare out their tail feathers. They are usually seen alone and flit quickly between tree branches and headstones in pursuit of flying insects. Magpie robins are clever at using the cemetery resources for nesting. One nest was found in the crook of a marble angel's arm. The bowed head of the angel shielded the nest from sun and rain.

Bulbuls are more gregarious birds and feed in small groups. The most easily recognised are the crested and red-vented bulbuls; the former by its punk-like spike of feathers on its head and the latter by the patch of red on its rump. But by far the most fun are the cockatoos. They announce their arrival by ear-piercing squawks and usually travel in gangs. They often visit the Lychee tree when the fruits are in season, their big beaks snipping off small twigs and leaves that rain down on the path below. Cockatoos are not native to Hong Kong and it is said that the two or three colonies of them that inhabit the wooded hillsides of Hong Kong Island are descendents of cockatoos released from an aviary just before the Japanese occupation during World War II.

Spotted doves and sparrows are very common throughout the urban areas. In the cemetery, the doves feed mainly on the ground in the grass around the headstones. Their sudden loud-flapping take-offs can be startling in the quiet of the cemetery. Sparrows are small and inconspicuous but can also delight the cemetery visitor with a thrilling display of aerobatics chasing and catching a moth or butterfly in flight. Look out too for fledgeling birds in spring learning to fly and hunt.

Stop 13: **HMS** *Calcutta* **monument**

Continuing along the curved path, it is impossible to miss the huge military monument on the right erected by the admiral, officers and crew of HMS *Calcutta* in memory of shipmates who died whilst the ship was on active duty in China waters between 1856 and 1860. The scale of this monument, built from bulky granite building blocks, is in keeping with HMS *Calcutta* which weighed in at an impressive 2,299 tons and had such a deep draught that it could not sail up the Pearl River. Like a box tomb, the monument is constructed with a hollow interior and its stability depends on the stonemason's skill at fitting the walls and roof panels snugly together. Not surprisingly, the sheer weight of the stonework has contributed to uneven settlement over time causing gaps to open up between blocks. The largest fissures have been filled with conspicuous cement repairs. This is only a temporary measure since rain penetration will exacerbate the problem and, sooner rather than later, this monument will need some serious foundation and stabilisation work to prevent collapse. Note the symbolic broken cannon on one of the side panels.

Stop 14: **Sir Robert Ho Tung**

Nearby, in complete contrast to the rather dilapidated HMS *Calcutta* monument, is a pair of pristine white marble crosses. The crosses mark the graves of Sir Robert Ho Tung (1862–1956) and his first wife Lady Margaret Mak Sau Ying (1865–1944). A few feet in front is a simple white marble tablet headstone that marks the grave of Au Shing Cheung, Lady Margaret's faithful servant for over forty years. This prominent placement of Au Shing Cheung's grave is a mark of respect by her former employers. Ho Tung was Eurasian, born to an English father and Chinese mother. After graduating from Queen's College he worked as a clerk for the Chinese Imperial Maritime Customs in Guangzhou, returning in 1880 to join the British-owned trading company Jardine Mathieson. He advanced quickly, thanks to his bilingual and business skills, and became director of many Hong Kong companies, including Hong Kong Land. Ho Tung was also a philanthropist, supporting many charitable organisations including the Tung Wah Hospital. Being Eurasian, he encountered racial prejudice and during his life he did much to redress this, notably establishing the Chinese Club (since the Hong Kong Club did not admit Chinese members) and being the first Eurasian to live on the Peak (previously prohibited by the British).

Stop 15: Sir Paul Catchick Chater

Slightly downhill from Ho Tung's memorial is another marble cross with edged compound in memory of Sir Paul Catchick Chater (1846–1926). Chater's life story is one of stunning business success, generous philanthropy and playing an integral part in almost every aspect of Hong Kong life. Chater had a very humble upbringing; born in Calcutta to a family of Armenian merchants, one of fourteen children and sadly orphaned at the age of nine. Despite this early setback, Chater was educated on a scholarship and, at the age of eighteen, came to Hong Kong to work in the Bank of Hindustan, China and Japan. Business was his forte and within a couple of years he had left the bank to become a successful bullion exchange trader and land investor. By the 1880s, Chater was closely involved in almost all major business ventures in Hong Kong ranging from insurance, land reclamation, shipping and utilities. He amassed great wealth and gave generously to many organisations and good causes including Hong Kong University, St John's Cathedral and St Andrew's Church in Kowloon. He was a long serving member of the Executive Council, a prominent member of the freemasons and was mentor to many other entrepreneurs at the time including Robert Ho Tung. Local landmarks bearing his name include Chater Garden and Chater Road. They are small tokens of appreciation of Sir Paul's achievements and Hong Kong owes him a great debt for his insight, courage, business acumen and generosity.

Stop 16: Frangipani tree (*Plumeria rubra var. acutifolia*)

Continuing downhill, at the next path intersection, there is a large Frangipani tree that sheds its exotic fragrant flowers over the nearby graves. The tradition of planting flowering trees in the cemetery originates from the difficulty for distant relatives to visit graves of loved ones. Each year the trees scatter flowers over the graves on their behalf. Unfortunately, the same tree is making the adjacent headstone lean precariously. Apart from the pronounced tilt, this memorial is also noteworthy for its distinctive Russian Orthodox cross — two horizontal bars and a third one set at an angle. Before moving on, stand for a moment at the footpath intersection and take in the panorama of the different memorials and cultures in view. The cemetery is like a microcosm of Hong Kong as a cultural crossroads. In addition to the Russian Orthodox crosses there are Celtic crosses (favoured by Scots and Irish), polished black granite obelisks (favoured by Germans), exquisitely carved white marble angels, stolid granite military monuments, delicate cherubs on children's graves and a couple of makeshift designs from welded pipes and timber.

Stop 17: Polish timber cross

Possibly the most vulnerable memorial in the cemetery is a small timber cross located beside the path a few metres downhill from the Frangipani tree. It is easy to miss and the painted lettering has weathered away. Fragments of the lettering, recorded in a photograph taken in 2001, suggest that the deceased was Polish and died in the 1920s. In time, weather and termites will make the timber disintegrate and it would be nice to think that, before this happens, a simple plaque or replacement cross, inscribed with details of the deceased from the cemetery office records, could be erected.

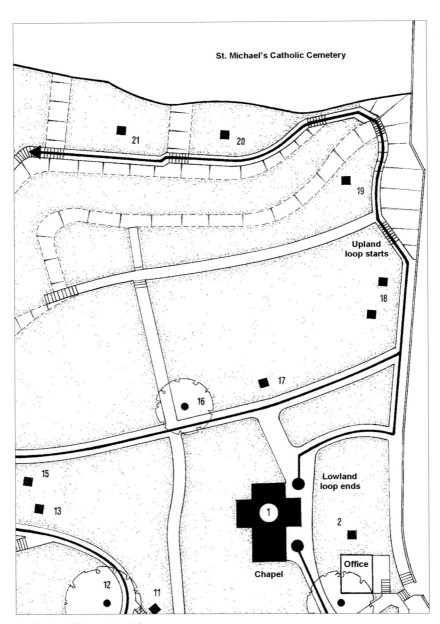

St. Michael's Catholic Cemetery

21

20

19

Upland
loop starts

18

17

16

15

13

Lowland
loop ends

1

2

Office

Chapel

12

11

Guide Map 3 (Stops 18 to 21)

SELF-GUIDED TOUR

Stop 18: Nautical memorials and slate plaques

Downhill from the timber cross there are some very sturdy granite memorials with a nautical design. These include one shaped like a capstan (the winch on a ship's deck used to wind up the anchor) and others with anchor motifs. With Hong Kong being a coastal city, it is understandable that a large number of sailors are buried in the Hong Kong Cemetery and memorials should bear seafaring symbols. The anchor is a very common icon which symbolises Christian faith and hope which is steadfast in the face of death. The key Bible reference for this is Hebrews 6:19: 'We have this hope as an anchor for the soul, firm and secure.'

There are also good examples of slate plaques laid into recesses of two of these granite memorials. Slate is a metamorphic rock formed primarily by extreme heat and pressure on fine-grained clays. Unlike the other more common memorial materials in the cemetery (granite and marble) slate can be engraved with very fine copperplate lettering and crisp detailing. It is very resistant to weathering and the dense, fine-grained surface generally remains clear of organic growths. When slate does deteriorate it usually does so by delaminating in thin layers, betraying its sedimentary clay origins. The cause is usually weathering out of softer portions of carbonates or clay minerals. Also, chemical reactions with iron pyrites in the slate may result in crumbly rust patches and deep holes in the stone. Slate is normally used in thin sections which can crack if mishandled. It is therefore very important to remove any tree seedlings from slate plaque joints promptly.

This completes the tour of the lowland portion of the cemetery. To follow the extended tour which explores the upper portion of the cemetery take the flight of steps to the next platform.

Stop 19: Sir Kai Ho Kai

The memorial to Sir Kai Ho Kai (1859–1914) is an interesting mix of different coloured marbles and includes a relatively detailed engraved epitaph to his considerable achievements. Ho Kai was born in Hong Kong to a family of eleven children and had a Western education in law and medicine. His father, Ho Fuk-tong, had a dual career of Anglican minister and real estate tycoon. With Ho Kai's family and educational background it is not surprising that he became a skilled intermediary between the government and the Chinese people in Hong Kong, speaking out strongly on a number of social issues such as the evils of gambling and opium addiction. His impressive career included being the first Chinese to qualify in medicine, the second Chinese barrister admitted to the Supreme Court of Hong Kong and the third Chinese to be a member of the Legislative Council. Despite his long service as a Legco member, some questioned his loyalty to the colonial government due to his close associations with Sun Yat Sen and the revolutionary thought of the time.

Ho Kai pioneered the introduction of training in Western medicine in Hong Kong and was very generous with his financial assistance to those in need. However, his business career proved to be less successful. An example was his joint investment with his business partner Au Tak in a parcel of land in Kowloon for real estate development. The money ran out and the government bought the land for a small military and civilian airfield. This land was later to become Hong Kong's international airport and was named after the two original investors — Kai Tak.

Ho Kai's memorial is interesting from another aspect in that it narrowly escaped being badly damaged by a falling granite obelisk. The obelisk still lies in the grass nearby and a close inspection of its base and the plinth it fell from shows that no metal dowels were installed to hold it secure. The obelisk was merely balanced on the plinth with a thin skin of cement to hold it in place. A good design would have had at least three aligned holes drilled into the connecting surfaces of the column and plinth. Strong iron dowels would have been set into the holes using molten lead and the two parts fixed together. Repairs today would use modern materials such as stainless steel dowels and epoxy adhesive. This is a useful reminder that some craftsmen and contractors cut corners in the past just as they do today and that memorial columns should not be rocked to test if they are wobbly — they very likely are!

Stop 20: Spelling mistakes

In May 2007, examples of blatant misspelling of painted inscriptions on some military headstones in the Hong Kong Cemetery, as well as botched repairs to the stonework, were noticed and criticised in the media. The British Ministry of Defence admitted it was the fault of their contractor. Some of the worst examples can be seen in this portion of the cemetery.

Apart from human error, the natural weathering of the headstones, particularly those made from local granite, is a contributing factor. Granite is an igneous rock produced by the slow cooling of magma beneath the Earth's crust resulting in a medium to coarse-grained rock that is relatively durable but difficult to carve in fine detail. It has a typically speckled crystalline appearance, comprising mainly mica, feldspar and quartz. If given a polished finish, granite can stand up well to weathering and requires minimum maintenance. However, one common problem is that the impact of machine tooling may leave a network of hairline cracks in the surface layer of stone which in time may disintegrate by scaling or flaking.

In addition, the crystalline structure means that, over time, natural weathering of the surface can result in small particles of stone crumbling off. In heavily polluted cities such as Hong Kong, granites may also be seriously damaged if they contain pyrites or sulphides such as iron or copper sulphide. These materials may react with sulphuric acid in precipitation (acid rain) and cause staining or disintegration of the stone matrix.

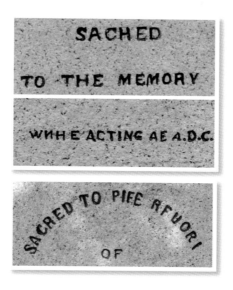

Depending upon the location of such flaws and the depth of the carving, this can, for example, make letters like 'F' change to a 'P' or an 'R' look more like a 'B'. This is not usually a major problem as common sense can determine the correct spelling but it becomes an issue when some well-meaning individual subsequently paints the letters to clarify the inscription but highlights the wrong letter. Painting headstone inscriptions does no significant damage to the stone itself. Indeed, anyone who has visited a local Chinese cemetery during the *Ching Ming* or *Chung Yeung* grave-sweeping festivals will know that repainting the inscribed characters is often one of the rituals observed. However, to avoid embarrassing bloopers, it is important to understand that natural weathering may obscure the lettering and, if in doubt, the painter should seek advice from a native speaker of the language of the inscription. A fundamental guiding principle for good conservation practice is never to guess.

Stop 21: Yeung Kui Wan

One of the prominent supporters of Dr Sun Yat Sen's revolution against the Qing government was Yeung Kui Wan (1861–1901). Sun and Yeung met frequently with co-conspirators in secret locations in Hong Kong to talk politics and tactics. In 1895 Yeung was elected chairman of the Xingzhonghui (Revive China Society), chief commander of the Canton Uprising and president of the provisional government. As Sun Yat Sen's right-hand man, Yeung played a strategic part in the revolutionary plans. This made him a target for enemy agents and on 10 January 1901 he was assassinated in Gage Street beside his old school. His family, fearing that his grave would be desecrated by his murderers, chose to erect it with no inscription. Today, it still stands anonymously in a quiet corner of the cemetery — the only risk now being the overhanging branch of a mature Chinese banyan tree that threatens to knock the obelisk over in the next typhoon.

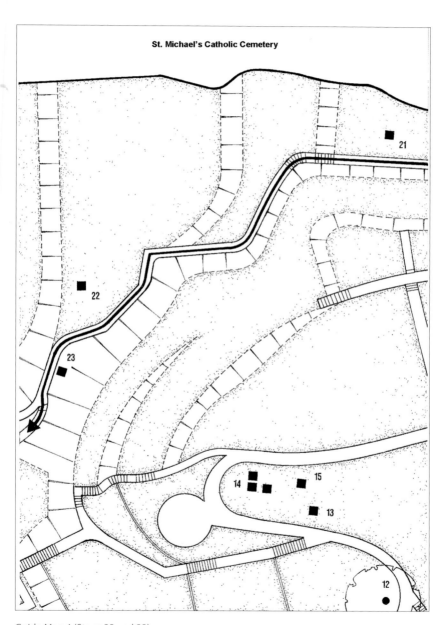

St. Michael's Catholic Cemetery

SELF-GUIDED TOUR

Guide Map 4 (Stops 22 and 23)

Stop 22: Constable Ernest Goucher

The memorial to Constable Ernest Goucher (1894–1915) can be difficult to find being located among rows of similar tablet headstones dedicated to former members of the police force: count six in from the path along the row second from the back.

In the early 1900s, tigers were a threat to villagers in the New Territories. To help deter tiger attacks, it was customary for villagers walking along country tracks to travel in pairs or groups. The year 1915 appears to have been a particularly bad year for tigers. One terrorised residents on the Peak for months. Another was spotted by villagers in the Fanling and Sheung Shui area who reported the sighting to sceptical police officers in Fanling Police Station.

The *South China Morning Post* reported the next day (9 March 1915) that two officers (Sergeant Goucher and Constable Hollands) went to investigate armed with only a regular shotgun and revolver. As they approached the area indicated by the villagers, the tiger charged from thick undergrowth and mauled Sergeant Goucher, breaking his arm and deeply gashing his back. Constable Hollands emptied his revolver into the tiger's flank and, although the bullets did not inflict a fatal wound, the tiger let the sergeant go. Goucher was taken to hospital in Kowloon by a special train but, as his headstone records, died of his wounds a few days later. The wounded tiger killed another policeman, Constable Rutton Singh, in the next hunting party but was eventually shot and killed by police marksmen. The tiger's stuffed head as well as the photograph below are on display at the Police Museum on Coombe Road with a caption that records the tiger (*Panthera Tigris Tigris* — Bengal tiger) measured 8 feet 6 inches long (2.59 metres) and weighed 289 pounds (131 kilograms).

It is interesting to note that the *SCMP* report states the first police officer who died from his injuries to be Sergeant Goucher. Sharp-eyed readers will note that the headstone records his rank as constable. The Police Museum's tiger exhibit states that both Goucher and Hollands were constables. This suggests that details reported in newspapers need to be double-checked and that the rush to get fresh copy to press can lead to errors. By contrast, a headstone takes time to carve and, in the case of a policeman, would be carefully checked by fellow officers in addition to relatives and friends. The value of the cemetery's ten thousand or so headstones as accurate and reliable historical records should never be underestimated.

During a visit to the cemetery with staff of Kadoorie Farm it was pointed out that Constable Goucher's epitaph has considerable educational value to convince school children brought up in Hong Kong's urban jungle that there used to be tigers here.

The Fanling Tiger. Reproduced with the kind permission of the Hong Kong Public Records Office.

Stop 23: Upland Woodland Habitat

This section of the upland loop is quite different in character to the open sunny lawns and ornamental clipped shrubs in the lowland portion of the cemetery. The formed platforms are quite narrow and shaded by dense copses of mature woodland trees growing on the intervening steep slopes. Having just read about tiger attacks, a sudden rustle in the tangled undergrowth nearby can give you goose bumps. If it is not the wind it is most likely a coucal — a bold black and rust coloured bird that likes to root around in shrubbery and is a common visitor to this part of the cemetery.

Where the memorials are in perpetual shade under the tree canopies, moss or orange-grey coloured algae grow on the headstones. In some cases, this can obscure the inscription. Some built heritage conservation experts will say that this should all be cleaned off while nature conservationists will argue that some insects such as moths feed on this kind of plant and it should not be removed. A reasonable compromise would be to gently clean off the vegetative growth on the inscription but leave it intact elsewhere on the headstone.

Continue uphill for a few metres then take the left fork, shown in the photograph. Descend the steps and follow the grassy track to Stop 24.

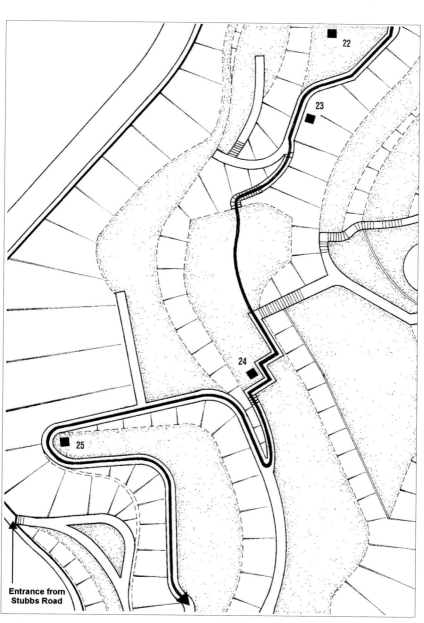

Guide Map 5 (Stops 24 and 25)

Stop 24: Corporal Joseph Hughes

Corporal Joseph Hughes (1925–46) was a 20-year-old from Glasgow stationed with the Army Service Corps at Lyemun Barracks. One of the Corps' assignments was to help in removing unexploded ordinance and disused ammunition left behind after World War II. On the morning of 21 March 1946, Hughes was driving a lorry loaded with explosives and ordinance back to the barracks. Before he reached his destination, Hughes noticed that the back of the lorry was on fire and the load was in imminent danger of blowing up. He bravely decided to stay with the lorry and succeeded in steering it away from heavily populated areas. Unfortunately, he was killed when it exploded before he could stop and get clear himself. On 26 June 1947, Hughes was awarded the George Cross posthumously for his selfless bravery. The George Cross is the highest British military honour that can be awarded for valour in peacetime.

Stop 25: Memorial with swastika motif

One of the most surprising icons to be seen in the cemetery is a German swastika on a granite headstone dated 30 December 1934. The inscription is in German and, although indistinct in places, suggests it is the grave of a sailor from a German ship that visited Hong Kong. The swastika emblem has had a deep religious meaning to many cultures, particularly Buddhists and Hindus, for over three thousand years. Hitler adopted the swastika as the official emblem of the Nazi Party at the Salzburg Conference on 7 August 1920. Thereafter, it was common for military personnel to wear the swastika insignia to symbolise national pride and unity, which helps explain its use on a sailor's headstone in Hong Kong dated 1934, five years before the outbreak of World War II. Today, the symbol is associated worldwide with the Nazi holocaust atrocities and arouses feelings of deep-rooted anger, hatred and disgust.

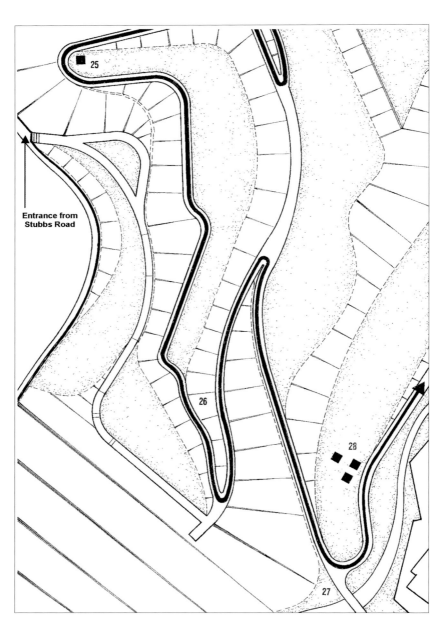

Guide Map 6 (Stops 26 to 28)

Stop 26: Shotcrete slopes versus vegetation

It is unfortunate that, over time, some of the steep vegetated slopes of the cemetery have been replaced by a skin of sprayed concrete (shotcrete). This portion of the cemetery is a good example of how ugly this kind of engineered slope treatment can look. At the time of writing, more slope stabilisation works are in progress around the cemetery and will likely result in a net loss of slope vegetation. Government bodies such as the Geotechnical Engineering Office and Civil Engineering Development Department advocate use of 'green' slope treatments to replace shotcrete and the cemetery management (Food and Environmental Hygiene Department) should ensure any contractor working on slope works in the cemetery follows GEO's and CEDD's guidelines. For example, if the slope is just too steep to support soil and plants, then one of the simplest techniques is to use natural granite blocks to cover the face of the slope and install a planter along the bottom edge. The planter only needs to hold enough soil for low-maintenance climbing plants such as ivy (*Parthenocissus himalayana*) and in a few growing seasons the slope will be green again.

Stop 27: Stream course and wildlife

Descending back into the woodland fringe, pause on the bridge spanning the natural stream in the shade of the two large Chinese banyan trees (*Ficus microcarpa*). This is a good vantage point to spot butterflies as they generally prefer the woodland fringe where they can take advantage of the dappled shade on hot days. Dragonflies can also be seen in good numbers in and around the stream course and woodland fringe. They prey on mosquitoes and are a welcome sight to visitors who are prone to mosquito bites. Common mosquito repellents available on the market include citronella-scented patches and ultrasonic wrist band devices. The sound emitted from the latter is intended to imitate the rhythm of a dragonfly's wing beat. Also look out for well-camouflaged lizards that like to sun themselves on the rocks beside the stream.

Stop 28: Three obelisks

Grouped together in a corner of the path are three large pyramidal granite obelisks. These monuments once stood in prominent road junctions in the urban area but were all relocated to the cemetery because, as the city developed, they started to obstruct the traffic. They all commemorate seamen who lost their lives in Hong Kong and China waters as a result of illness, battles or natural disaster.

- Crew of HMS *Vestal* who died from accidents (falling from height or drowning), in action or other unspecified reasons from 1844 to 1847. This obelisk was originally located at the junction of Queen's Road East and Wong Nei Chung Road.

- Crew of the United States Steam Frigate *Powhatan* and Steam Sloop *Rattler* who fell in a combined boat attack on a fleet of piratical junks off Kuhlan, 4 August 1855. This obelisk was originally located in Leighton Road.

- Crew of the Torpedo Boat Destroyer *Fronde* who died in the typhoon that hit Hong Kong on 18 September 1906. This obelisk was originally located at the junction of Jordan Road and Gascoigne Road.

Of the three, the HMS *Vestal* obelisk was perhaps the best known and was nicknamed 'The Monument'. It was a popular gathering point for mourners who wished to join funeral processions that passed by on the way to the cemetery. It is unfortunate that the decision was made to place the obelisks so close together. A better arrangement would have been to erect them at major footpath junctions within the lowland area of the cemetery where they could be appreciated as originally intended.

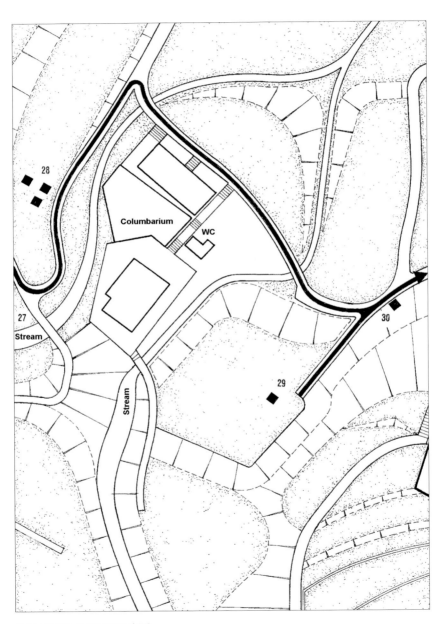

Guide Map 7 (Stops 29 and 30)

Stop 29: Memorial with decorative ironwork

The metal fence that surrounds this memorial is one of the best examples of decorative ironwork in Hong Kong. The memorial itself is a polished black granite bodystone which once had lead lettering set into the surface. This may be a German memorial as almost all the other polished black granite memorials in the cemetery have German inscriptions. The lettering was most likely removed during World War II because of its value as a raw material to barter for food or other essentials for survival during those terrible times. However, the exquisite wrought and cast iron decorative perimeter railings have survived virtually intact.

The delicately shaped flowers, fruits and leaves are cast iron, i.e., made from pouring molten iron into moulds. This is only commercially viable if many castings are to be made and, therefore, this railing design was most likely a funerary catalogue product. The bars of the railings and curved/spiral plant stems are wrought iron, i.e., cut and bent by hand in a blacksmith's forge. The individual components of the railings would have been riveted and clamped together in conveniently sized panels that would be packed and shipped to Hong Kong for final assembly in the cemetery.

Both cast iron and wrought iron are durable materials if properly maintained, e.g., by regular painting. However, if neglected they will rust. When the iron is set into a stone base (traditionally with a lead seal) any water penetration into the stone cavity may result in the iron rusting. As it rusts, the iron expands and will eventually crack the stone. Also, cast iron has a high carbon content that makes it relatively brittle and prone to breakage when subjected to a blow or bending forces from, say, uneven ground settlement under the memorial.

Stop 30: **Bat roosts**

While touring the cemetery, keep a close lookout for bat roosts. During a visit with Dr Gary Ades, a leading expert in bats at Kadoorie Farm, Dr Ades spotted a roost of dog-faced fruit bats in the crown of a nearby Chinese Fan Palm (*Livistona chinensis*). Bats like the Chinese Fan Palm (*right photograph*) because they can nibble partly through the ribs on the palm fronds so that they bend over and provide better protection from the sun and rain. This bat species also likes to roost in locations close to their food source — in this case a Common Red-stem Fig tree (*Ficus variegata var. chlorocarpa*). Bats are auspicious in Chinese culture and play a vital role in the cemetery ecosystem. Depending on the species, they pollinate flowers, spread fruit seeds and can devour as many as three thousand mosquitoes in one night. To avoid using insecticides in the cemetery a more environmentally friendly method to control mosquitoes would be to help nurture the insectivore bat population by installing bat boxes and opening up a small access for bats to make use of the derelict air raid tunnel beside the path.

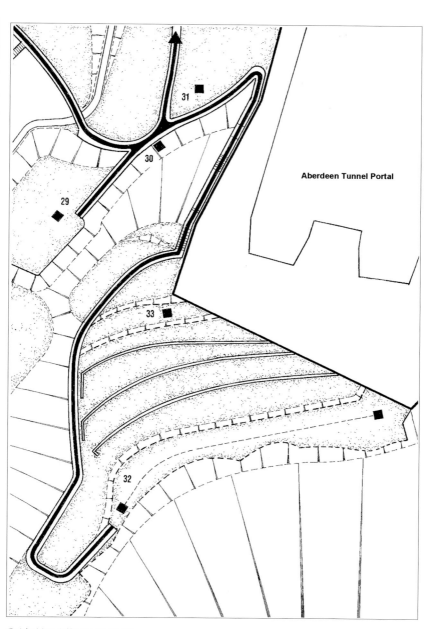

Aberdeen Tunnel Portal

Guide Map 8 (Stops 31 to 33)

Stop 31: Children's memorials

Close by the derelict air raid tunnel is one of the sections in the cemetery devoted to children's memorials. The sight of these small graves with the downsized headstones never fails to humble the visitor and one can imagine the love, sorrow and anguish in the hearts of the parents who laid their children to rest here. This area contains one of the most beautifully carved marble headstones in the cemetery depicting winged cherubs and roses. Winged cherubs are diminutive angelic figures that represent the soul of the deceased soaring to heaven. The roses, which would have been white before the marble became discoloured by pollution, symbolise the purity of the children.

Stops 32 and 33: Japanese memorials and the cherry tree trail

Near to the children's memorials, at a bend in the path, is a small cherry tree. Follow the path uphill from here and keep a lookout for more recently planted cherry trees at strategic corners in the path. These trees mark the way to the section where most of the Japanese memorials are located. The trees (fourteen in all) were planted, with the cemetery management's permission, on 14 February 2004 by the Hong Kong Japanese Club with the help of students from local Japanese high schools. Each spring, a group of around one hundred students return with the Japanese Club to sweep the graves. It is a welcome example of care and attention to the cemetery that is, with a few exceptions, sadly missing elsewhere. The inscription on the banner shown in the photograph reads, 'Memorial Service Venue, Hong Kong Japanese Club, 14 March 2009'.

The Japanese memorials are easily identified by their simple, square, columnar shape and date from 1878 to 1945. This design is believed to originate from around one thousand years ago during the Heian Period (AD 794–1185) when a simpler style was advocated. Earlier headstones used to be similar to the Chinese tablet form.

The memorials are typically for merchants, sailors and nurses who had emigrated to or were passing through Hong Kong. One memorial stands separate from the others (*right photograph, Stop 33*) on a lower platform and was erected in the early 1900s to commemorate the *karayuki-san* (literally 'Ms Gone-overseas'). The *karayuki-san* were young women from poor farming or fishing communities who had been sold into the local sex trade during the Meiji (1868–1912) and Taisho Periods (1912–1926). A sampling of the memorial inscriptions indicates that some came from Amakusa in the Kumamoto Prefecture in Kyushu, which is known to have been the hometown of many *karayuki-san*.

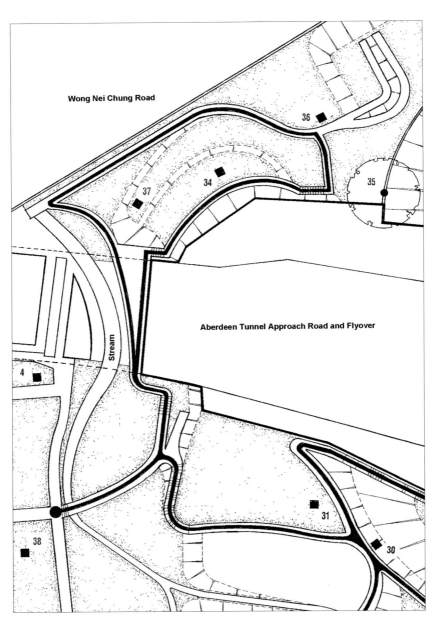

Guide Map 9 (Stops 34 to 38)

Stop 34: Stonemason's nightmare

The walk under the highway flyover is unpleasant but thankfully short. In contrast, the memorial to Sergeant James Walsh, erected in 1868, illustrates a nightmare that must haunt stonemasons to their dying day — spotting a glaring spelling or grammatical mistake after a headstone is carved. On this memorial, the phrase 'Who Departed Life' should have read 'Who Departed This Life'. The clumsy insertion of 'This' into the line is most unusual. Was the error made by the client in penning the original text and the stonemason balked at redoing the whole engraving? Did the stonemason make the mistake on his own, distracted perhaps by a lunch break between carving 'Departed' and 'Life'? Or, maybe the original text had a handwritten insert just like it appears on the stone and the stonemason merely copied faithfully what was given to him? Whatever the reason, the result is a charming reminder of our human fallibility. This memorial faces away from the path and will need a little more effort to locate: count twelve back from the far end of the second row.

Stop 35: Big-leaved Fig Tree (*Ficus virens var. sublanceolata*)

The sixth and last 'Old and Valuable Tree' in the cemetery is the Big-leaved Fig that is growing on and over a stone retaining wall. The eye-catching spread of buttress roots is typical of other fig trees such as the Chinese banyan and the broad canopy casts a perpetual shadow over the nearby memorials. The Big-leaved Fig tree is native to Hong Kong. It is semi-deciduous and extremely hardy, producing several crops of figs a year that appear dark purple when ripe. Given its location on the wall it was clearly not deliberately planted by cemetery garden staff but is self-seeded, aided by birds or fruit bats who enjoy the figs.

Stop 36: **Fallen memorials**

The cluster of three damaged memorials by the side of the path illustrates the danger of neglecting maintenance of the cemetery's built heritage resources. As the square obelisk fell from its plinth (no securing dowel pins evident) it toppled an adjacent tablet headstone then knocked a chunk off a second memorial before coming to rest face down in the grass. This was first noted during a cemetery visit in 2002 and, to date, nothing has been done to stabilise the fallen stonework let alone repair the damage and reinstate the obelisk and headstone to their original positions.

Once a headstone falls over, either face up or down, it is vulnerable to accelerated deterioration. If left lying face up, water will gather in the grooves of the engraving and encourage mosquito breeding as well as growth of mould and moss. Like acid rain, the acidity of vegetation is particularly damaging to marble headstones and attacks the joints between the calcite crystals. If left face down, the stone will tend to stain from prolonged contact with the ground and, of course, will be illegible to passers-by.

Stop 37: Plant damage

Within sight of the 'Old and Valuable' Big-leaved Fig tree, described at Stop 35, is another fig with roots that are rapidly enveloping a nearby memorial. This kind of tree may look good on a granite retaining wall but is obviously inappropriate close to memorials. Again, it appears to be self-seeded but its growth has gone unchecked for decades. The cemetery maintenance teams need to be briefed to remove any seedlings that pop up between memorials as well as in stonework joints to prevent similar damage occurring elsewhere. Part of the problem is that this portion of the cemetery is cut off from the other areas thanks to the Aberdeen Tunnel and flyover construction in the mid-1970s. As a result, it is less frequented by visitors and suffers from some of the worst examples of maintenance neglect.

Stop 38: Military war graves

The final stop is at one of the sections dedicated to military memorials. The most common stone used is Portland Stone — a creamy white stone quarried in England. There is a variety of different designs but the simple tablet with slightly arched top is the one most commonly used here and in other cemeteries around the world for British and Commonwealth soldiers, sailors and airmen. Some minor variations in detailing can be noted to distinguish between different branches of the armed services. However, the principle is that the memorials are similar, regardless of rank. The regular columns and rows of matching headstones evoke an image of a well-drilled platoon standing to attention.

Each year on Remembrance Sunday (the second Sunday of November), wreaths of red poppies are laid beside the memorials as a mark of respect by relatives and local representatives of the Commonwealth War Graves Commission. The Commission oversees repairs and cleaning of the military headstones. The origin of the red poppies dates from World War I (1914–18) when hundreds of thousands of troops were massacred in France in trench battles. Poppies grew in profusion in the fields of Flanders where many of the dead soldiers were buried. The imagery of the blood red poppies growing

SELF-GUIDED TOUR

between the soldiers' graves, as well as the death of a close friend, inspired a Canadian military doctor, Major John McCrae, to write the following poem in 1915 during the Second Battle of Ypres.

> In Flanders fields the poppies blow
> Between the crosses, row on row,
> That mark our place; and in the sky
> The larks, still bravely singing, fly
> Scarce heard amid the guns below.
>
> We are the Dead. Short days ago
> We lived, felt dawn, saw sunset glow,
> Loved and were loved, and now we lie
> In Flanders fields.
>
> Take up our quarrel with the foe:
> To you from failing hands we throw
> The torch; be yours to hold it high.
> If ye break faith with us who die
> We shall not sleep, though poppies grow
> In Flanders fields.

It is fitting to complete the tour here as these military memorials set an excellent example of how the rest of the cemetery might look if the civilian memorials could be afforded the same level of respect, protection and care. Further reading on the people and events introduced on the tour can be found in the chapter notes.[3]

Footnote

Having completed the tour, it may come as a surprise that the Hong Kong Cemetery does not have any official status or protection as a heritage site. There has never been a comprehensive condition survey of the heritage resources described above and there is no conservation management plan for the ten thousand irreplaceable headstones or diverse flora and fauna. If you feel strongly about the safety or neglect of the memorials seen on the tour or any other conservation issue relating to the cemetery please take the time to write to the Development Bureau to voice your concern.

5 Last Words

Up until now, heritage conservation work in Hong Kong has been carried out in a rather ad hoc manner. This is because, in the race against time, efforts have been focused on saving historical buildings threatened with demolition. There has not been a comprehensive approach to systematically assess and select heritage items for protection.

Home Affairs Bureau[1]

The ensemble of four cemeteries in Happy Valley is a very significant historic cultural landscape. Individually, the cemeteries are important to the cultural identity of different minority religions: Muslim, Catholic, Protestant and Parsee. Collectively, they are a microcosm of Hong Kong's cultural and religious diversity.

Of the four, Hong Kong Cemetery expresses the nineteenth-century European cemetery garden concept most clearly; accommodating tasteful memorials in an attractive park setting that is respectful to the dead and inspirational to visitors. Established in 1845, it is the oldest and largest cemetery in the ensemble. It contains the oldest surviving colonial building and public fountain in Hong Kong and its garden has matured into a rich wildlife habitat. The memorials provide a valuable and continuous historic timeline of the evolution of Hong Kong society, faithfully recording the lives, hardships and deaths of the civilian community as well as military personnel during the colonial era — a distinct and very influential period in Hong Kong's history.

However, all is not well. The condition of numerous memorials has deteriorated badly and urgent remedial action is required. This final chapter will suggest the way forward to pro-actively conserve the valuable built and natural heritage resources in the Hong Kong Cemetery following three basic steps:

1. Protection of the cemetery as an historic cultural landscape
2. Preparation of a detailed conservation plan
3. Participation of various stakeholder groups

Protection of the cemetery as an historic cultural landscape

The vital first step is for the government to acknowledge that the cemetery has so far been overlooked as a site of heritage significance and put in place an effective means of statutory protection. The existing land use zoning of 'Other Uses (Cemetery)' proved to be no deterrent to the construction of a tunnel and highway through the heart of the site in the 1970s. To prevent similar insensitive and destructive development, the cemetery needs to be designated as an historic cultural landscape, i.e., a heritage site comprising the chapel, memorials and flora and fauna habitats as one entity.

What may have prevented this being done to date is that, in Hong Kong, heritage conservation tends to be divided into two main streams: built heritage (monuments and buildings) and natural heritage (flora and fauna). Adopting one or the other approach to protect the site would be inadequate because the Hong Kong Cemetery comprises a complex mix of built and natural heritage resources and needs a form of statutory protection that combines both aspects.

Earlier chapters discussed how the Hong Kong Cemetery was influenced by the nineteenth-century cemetery garden movement of which Père Lachaise Cemetery and the Glasgow Necropolis played such a major role. These historic cemetery gardens are also under government management. How are they protected?

Père Lachaise Cemetery is subject to several legal and regulatory protection measures, relating as much to built as to natural heritage aspects. The oldest part of the cemetery (43 hectares — about half the total site) has been classified as a significant site on the French government's List of Natural Monuments and Sites. The majority of this same portion of the cemetery (comprising tombs built before 1900) has also been declared an historic monument.[2]

In Glasgow, the whole of the Necropolis (15 hectares) is listed in the national Inventory of Gardens and Designed Landscapes and has been declared Grade B under the Statutory List of Buildings of Architectural or Historic Interest.[3] These lists are compiled by Scottish Natural Heritage and Historic Scotland respectively. The Grade B declaration means the site is of regional or more than local importance, or a major example of some particular period, style or building type, and should be preserved intact.

The importance of this comparison, apart from there being statutory protection securely in place, is that the protection for Père Lachaise and Glasgow Necropolis covers large areas (larger than the Hong Kong Cemetery's 10 hectares) comprising both built *and* natural heritage resources. Similar protection for the Hong Kong Cemetery should, therefore, be perfectly feasible.

Preparation of a detailed conservation plan for the cemetery

Assuming that the government is willing to take the first step and protect the cemetery as a site of built and natural heritage significance, the next step would be to prepare a detailed conservation plan to guide the site management team. This would entail carrying out detailed condition surveys of the memorials and flora and fauna habitats. However, by far the most important survey task to be carried out would be to identify the safety and stability of the memorials and establish a priority system for repairs.

Since the memorials are private property, the government has traditionally taken the stance that the owners are solely responsible for their upkeep. However, the memorials in most need of repair typically belong to foreigners who died here over a century ago and understandably left no twenty-first century forwarding address!

In the adjacent Happy Valley cemeteries (Muslim, Catholic and Parsee), the memorials are also private property but if a memorial falls into disrepair a different approach is adopted. A notice is posted in the cemetery requesting the owner to make the repairs. If the owners cannot be contacted and no-one responds to the notice within a given time, the management carries out the necessary repairs in the interests of safety as well as maintaining the cemetery in a neat and tidy condition. Ideally, the cost of the repairs is recovered from the owners. However, if this is not possible, the funds are drawn from the cemetery's maintenance budget.[4] A brief visit to any of the three cemeteries will confirm that this approach works — none has the air of neglect that currently hangs over the government-managed Hong Kong Cemetery.

In Père Lachaise and Glasgow Necropolis cemetery managers face additional challenges from vandals who spray graffiti on memorials or deliberately push them over. In the United Kingdom, reports of people being injured or killed in cemeteries by falling headstones are not uncommon. Although the victims are often the vandals themselves, who miscalculate the basic physics of large falling objects, accidents also happen on occasion to innocent visitors to the cemeteries who mistakenly lean against an unstable headstone. Since the cemeteries are open to the public, the management is vulnerable in these situations to being sued for injuries if the cemetery has not been kept in a safe condition.

In Glasgow Necropolis the city council recently completed a three-year programme to repair the memorials which had fallen into disrepair or had been abused by vandals. More refurbishment work is in the pipeline to help return the Necropolis to its former glory. Assistance from the National Lottery Fund is being sought to help finance this next phase of conservation work.[5] In the meantime, to help prevent any further vandalism, a ranger service has been provided to patrol the cemetery and provide guided tours. The new image of care and security that this creates has reduced the incidence of vandalism significantly, turning the cemetery from a potential eyesore to a source of civic pride.

Thankfully, vandalism is not prevalent in Hong Kong. Nevertheless, it would be preferable to check the Hong Kong Cemetery's memorials sooner rather than later and repair any unstable ones *before* rather than because someone is hurt.

One undesirable scenario is if the government responds to the need to check and stabilise memorials by simply locking the cemetery gates to keep the public out. Another is if suspect headstones are deliberately laid down flat or removed altogether instead of being repaired. If laid down, the headstones would soon stain from prolonged contact with the ground and inscriptions would either be illegible or weather more rapidly.

Preparing a detailed conservation plan is the only realistic way forward and would establish a clear plan of action and identify repair priorities. Memorials that need immediate attention would be highlighted and distinguished from those whose repairs were less urgent and could be attended to in phases spread over a number of years. For example, in Chapter 4, the leaning tablet headstone at Stop 11 would have a high priority for repair to prevent it from falling and causing injury or breaking. A memorial such as that shown at Stop 36, which has already toppled, broken and cannot fall any further, would be identified for repair as soon as possible once the high priority memorials were secure.

Other tour stops discussed a few simple preventive measures such as removal of tree seedlings from memorials (Stop 3) and more technical repairs such as re-erecting fallen obelisks and securing them with stainless steel dowels (Stop 19). Whatever the task, a high degree of skill and attention to detail is required to avoid damaging the memorials or their inscriptions. Excellent technical manuals for all types of memorial repairs have already been produced by various overseas heritage authorities, including Historic Scotland.[6]

It would be prudent to complement the conservation plan with a pilot study to test the various repair techniques to be used and establish the necessary standards and guidelines for contractors employed to carry out the work under the supervision of a heritage expert. To the east of the chapel is a section of memorials (including that of Gutzlaff) which would make an ideal pilot study as it is quite compact in size and contains a good cross-section of repair challenges including a fallen obelisk, leaning tablet headstone, rusting cast iron railings, and tree seedlings rooting into headstones.

The condition surveys of the flora and fauna would require a detailed ecological study covering all four seasons to determine how best to protect the cemetery's wildlife habitats. An important point not to lose sight of is that the rich biodiversity of the Hong Kong Cemetery has come about because of beneficial human intervention. The establishment of the cemetery garden and subsequent enrichment of plant species has, over time, attracted more wildlife than would otherwise have been there if the site had been left untouched. Normally, human intervention in a natural landscape results in a sharp decline in local biodiversity. It is rare to find a site like the Hong Kong Cemetery where the opposite is true.

Making the effort to understand the complex interrelationships between built and natural heritage elements is always worthwhile because it helps decision-makers to formulate more effective conservation guidelines. However, this is not always easy and can result in major disagreement between heritage experts. For example, in the UK, there has been much debate in recent years about which should take precedence: clear the vegetation and clean up the memorials or let nature take its course? Neither extreme is satisfactory and a sensible compromise is to identify different zones of management intensity.[7]

The Hong Kong Cemetery lends itself quite conveniently to this approach. The area covered by the lowland loop tour is the more formal portion of the cemetery. It contains the funeral chapel as a focal point and large areas of lawn, ornamental trees, shrubs and fountain, all of which influence visitors' first impressions of the cemetery. The level of maintenance needs to be highest here to ensure the memorials are in good condition, the grass is always cut, shrubs are clipped and any dead tree branches removed.

By contrast, the terraced landscape and winding paths of the upland loop are much less formal and the dense tree and shrub cover on the slopes between the terraces provide excellent cover for wildlife. It is still important to keep the grass on the terraces mown short — the last thing a visitor wants is to stub their toes on a concealed corner of a memorial or step on a snoozing snake. The woodland and scrub areas need a lighter touch by the maintenance team to prune back only what is necessary to keep the terraces clear and prevent overhanging tree branches from hitting memorials.

Management of the existing flora and fauna habitats means much more than just cutting the grass and brushing up fallen leaves. Trees will need replacement over time as the existing stock succumbs to old age, disease or typhoons. Good woodland management therefore involves a pro-active rolling programme of felling and new planting with the aim of sustaining and enhancing the overall biodiversity of the site. Whatever new planting is selected, it would do well to include species attractive to the bats and dragonflies that keep the mosquito numbers down.

Stop 23 on the upland loop tour highlights the problems of algae, lichens and mosses that can grow on headstones in areas shaded by trees and obscure the inscriptions. In the spirit of built versus natural heritage conservation compromise, if expert opinion suggests cleaning is feasible and justified, then good practice would be to clean only the inscription and leave the algae / lichen on the rest of the stone as it may be a food source for some species of insects such as moths.

Picking out an obscure or faint inscription with paint is possible but must be done with care or the existing problems of misspelling noted at Stop 20 would be exacerbated. Re-engraving a faint inscription on a memorial is not an option in heritage conservation and any temptation to do so should be vigorously resisted to protect the authenticity of the stonework. Instead, legible details of the inscription, in combination with archive record data, should be used to prepare a small plaque to be placed beside the headstone if desired.

A detailed conservation management plan would provide guidelines for all these issues. If such a plan had been prepared and implemented back in the early 1990s, in response to the Antiquities and Monuments Office's commissioned report by Bard on the cemetery's garrison graves, many of the problems highlighted on the tours in Chapter 4 could have been avoided or rectified by now.

Participation of various stakeholder groups

Although the Hong Kong Cemetery is often regarded as being exclusively for Western Protestants, its role has been to serve as a cemetery to any minority groups that have no cemetery to call their own. The cultural identity of the Muslim, Catholic and Parsee cemeteries is very clear-cut by comparison.

Statutory protection of the cemetery as a heritage site and preparation and implementation of a detailed conservation management plan should be the responsibility of the government since government is responsible for overall management of the site. However, once the necessary repairs to fallen or dangerous memorials have been completed, the third step would be to encourage the various stakeholder groups (churches, government departments and other associations) to become more involved in long-term care of the memorials.

The first phase make-over of the Glasgow Necropolis has resulted in renewed public interest and pride in the cemetery. The same could be true of the Hong Kong Cemetery. If the government were to start repairs to the memorials it would rekindle interest in the cemetery by like-minded conservation enthusiasts. Even just repairing the disused fountain and holding a small ceremony to mark the occasion would go a long way to starting this process.

The Commonwealth War Graves Commission already sets a good example by attending to the military graves each year in preparation for Remembrance Sunday in November (Stop 38). Several civilian memorials are also lovingly cared for by relatives. Examples highlighted on the tour are the white marble crosses marking the graves of Robert Ho Tung and his wife (Stop 14). In addition, several hundred Japanese memorials are cleaned each spring by a team of high school students organised by the Hong Kong Japanese Club (Stop 32). Perhaps the Hong Kong Police and Hong Kong Masonic Lodge could be persuaded to do the same for memorials of former members?

A major stakeholder in the Hong Kong Cemetery would be the Anglican Church due to the large proportion of Protestants buried there. In St. Michael's Catholic Cemetery next door, the Catholic Diocese takes pride in maintaining the memorials in good condition. It would be heart-warming if the Anglican Diocese were to consider, say, arranging volunteers to carry out periodic sprucing up of memorials in the Hong Kong Cemetery known to belong to former members of Anglican congregations. After all, the Anglican Church does have a legacy of helping to maintain the cemetery, started in the early 1860s by the Colonial Chaplain who used to turn his ponies into the cemetery to graze![8]

If such stakeholder groups, with or without their ponies, only manage an annual visit it would still make a huge difference to the appearance of the cemetery. An additional benefit of regular visits is that if a memorial is found to need repairs, instead of just being dusted down, it could be reported to the cemetery management promptly and the works slotted into the next phase of the repairs programme.

An important way of increasing public awareness of the heritage value of the cemetery and encourage stakeholder participation is by guided tours. This book is intended to provide a self-guided tour of the cemetery as it was originally designed to be experienced. That is, as a nineteenth-century meditative cemetery garden with a rich variety of built and natural heritage resources on display for the enjoyment and edification of the visitor.

Conclusion

There is a lot of urgent work to be done to prevent further loss of irreplaceable heritage resources in the Hong Kong Cemetery. I sincerely hope that this book will go some way to help change minds and spur the government on to be more pro-active and effective in conserving the cemetery for the education and enjoyment of future generations.

This is not a new quest. In November, 1865, an article in the *China Mail* made a similar plea for better treatment of the Happy Valley cemeteries with a very practical and surprisingly contemporary suggestion to help solve the problem.

The Cemeteries in the Happy Valley, though they may cease to be used, must ever remain undefiled. Let them be made an ornament and not a disfigurement to the place . . . It is much to be regretted that there are so few in the Colony to take an interest in preserving and beautifying the Cemeteries. Could not the Race Committee spare a few of the dollars that flow so plentifully into their coffers, for the purpose of improving the appearance of the site of their annual sports?[9]

But a word of warning is required. A heavy-handed or 'one-solution-suits-all' approach to a programme of restoration work would be disastrous. Those responsible for the conservation management of the cemetery need to have a subtle understanding of the heritage resources that, for example, distinguishes between the need to cut the grass and sweep up leaves but let the frangipani flowers that fall on the graves lie awhile. Similarly, if a bird builds a nest in the shelter of a memorial, leave it alone until after the young birds have flown. If this degree of sensitivity and understanding is applied, the future of the cemetery as a heritage treasure will be assured.

Fig. 5.1   Frangipani flowers on a child's grave

Fig. 5.2   Magpie Robin's nest on an angel's arm

Appendix 1
Glossary of Cemetery Icons

Anchor

With Hong Kong being a coastal city, it is understandable that a large number of sailors are buried in the Hong Kong Cemetery and memorials should bear seafaring symbols such as anchors or capstans (revolving drums used in raising or lowering anchors). The anchor is a symbol of hope and faithfulness. The key Biblical reference for this is Hebrews 6:19: 'Which hope we have as an anchor of the soul, both sure and steadfast.' An anchor was often the last hope for a sailor in a storm and the cemetery symbolism is that one's faith secured like an anchor in Christ will avoid a spiritual shipwreck. A variation on the anchor used in the cemetery is the anchor cross. It does not always have to mean that the deceased was a sailor. For example, to avoid persecution, early Christians used this disguised cross as a secret symbol. It is believed that the open curves of the base suggest the deceased was receptive towards spiritual matters.

Angel

Crosses and angels are perhaps the strongest images that a visitor to the cemetery will recall. Angels are considered in different religions and cultures to be God's messengers. The word angel comes from the Greek *angelos*, or messenger. In Islam, the word *mala'ika*, meaning messenger, is also the term for angel. However, despite frequent references to angels in the Bible, there is no detailed description of their physical appearance. Being regarded as messengers between Heaven and Earth, it is not surprising that they were believed to have wings, an image which was portrayed widely and refined during the Renaissance in church and religious art.

The angels in the Hong Kong Cemetery have a wide range of different expressions — some crouched over in grief, others looking or pointing heavenward with an expression of hope or joy. Cherubs are the diminutive angelic figures that are often seen on monuments for children. Winged cherubs are said to represent the soul of the deceased soaring to heaven.

Book

A book often represents the Bible. A closed book can have several meanings, such as virginity and mystery as well as the deceased having had a full life. An open book is an elegant way of recording the name of the deceased as well as symbolising a life being laid open honestly in the presence of the world and God.

Castle

A castle represents a stronghold for safe refuge and is intended to remind the observer of God's protection in times of strife. Psalm 59:16 illustrates the spiritual context of the castle symbol: 'But I will sing of your strength, in the morning I will sing of your love: for you are my fortress, my refuge in times of trouble.'

Column

Columns are visually striking features in the cemetery. Broken columns, in particular, became popular as funeral elements around the mid-1800s. They represent someone who died in their youth and, sadly, there are quite a few to be seen in the Hong Kong Cemetery — an indication of the numerous young British soldiers and sailors who died here in the difficult early years of the colony. Columns are sometimes decorated with urns, with or without shrouds. The shrouds usually represent the veil between earth and heaven. The urns are symbolic receptacles for the remains (ashes) of the deceased although, oddly, during the Victorian era when this decoration was most popular, full burial was much more common than cremation.

Cross

There are many different types of crosses to be found in the cemetery but the three most common are the Latin cross, Russian Orthodox cross and Celtic cross. The Latin cross is the simple, unadorned post and crossbar most commonly associated with Christianity. Some variations include the Cross of Calvary with a three-stepped base representing the Trinity of God the Father, Son and Holy Spirit; the Cross of Lorraine (after Godfrey of Lorraine, an early Crusader) which has a second shorter crossbar above the main crossbar; and the Crucifix which has the figure of Christ nailed to it.

The Russian Orthodox cross can be seen in many locations within the cemetery and is a variation of the cross of Lorraine with the addition of a third, angled crossbar below the main crossbar. Celtic crosses comprise a Latin cross with a circular section or nimbus at the intersection of the post and crossbar. They are commonly used by Scots or Irish as a symbol of national pride and are thought to have their origins in pagan pre-Christian times; one interpretation being the circle representing Mother Earth and the four arms of the cross being the four elements (air, earth, fire and water). Carvings on Celtic crosses can be intricate and richly detailed, knot patterns being commonly seen in the Hong Kong Cemetery examples.

Flora and fauna

Floral motifs became very popular in funeral art during the Victorian period, coinciding with the cemetery garden movement during the mid- to late 1800s. A special symbolism was attributed to each species of flower. Some of the most common ones that can be seen in the Hong Kong Cemetery include the following:

Acanthus: The Acanthus leaf is the detail used on the top of Corinthian columns. The leaves are prickly and symbolise the hardships endured during life on earth and the triumph of eternal life over death.

Clover: The three leaves of a clover or shamrock are used to symbolise the Trinity. It is said St. Patrick introduced this symbol to Ireland and the shamrock has been the country's emblem ever since.

Daisy: The simple daisy is often used to decorate the graves of children, symbolising the innocence and purity of the young souls.

Dove: The dove is the most common animal symbol seen in cemeteries and is often shown carrying an olive branch (see Olive description below). It is a symbol of purity and peace. When shown flying downwards the dove represents the Holy Ghost descending. This is described in the Bible (John 1:32) when John the Baptist baptises Jesus: 'I saw the Spirit come down from heaven as a dove and remain on him.'

Eagle: In the context of cemetery art, the eagle is a powerful image of the Resurrection and rebirth. This concept is derived from the legend that the eagle periodically flew towards the sun, burned its feathers, and plunged into the sea to save itself — similar to the act of baptism. Psalm 103: 4–5 describes this process of renewal: 'Who redeems your life from the pit and crowns you with love and compassion, who satisfies your desires with good things so that your youth is renewed like the eagle's.'

Fish: Christians first used a fish as their symbol before finally adopting the cross as their main emblem. The fish had several associations that made it a popular choice. The first disciples were fishermen and Christ told them to put aside their fishing nets and follow him to be 'fishers of men'. The Greek word for fish is *Icthus* — each letter being the first letters of the phrase 'Jesus Christ, of God, the Son, the Saviour'. The fish symbol was a useful secret code used by early Christians to avoid detection and persecution by the Roman authorities.

Grapes: Bunches of grapes represent the wine that is used during Holy Communion to remind Christians of Christ's blood shed on the cross to cleanse the sins of man. The grapevine is also a strong symbol in Christianity representing an intimate link between God and man. The Bible records Jesus' words to this effect in John 15:5, 'I am the vine, you are the branches. If a man remains in me and I in him, he will bear much fruit: apart from me you can do nothing.'

Ivy: Because ivy is a hardy evergreen plant it is associated with fidelity and immortality. It grows by clinging tightly to its support and is therefore a symbol of close and lasting friendship. In addition, the leaf has three points that are indicative of the Trinity — Father, Son and Holy Ghost.

Lamb: Christ is the Lamb of God, sacrificed to take away the sins of the world. Children's graves often show an image of a lamb which represents innocence. If the lamb is depicted with an accessory such as a cross, halo, shepherd's crook, alpha and omega lettering, it always represents the Lamb of God or Agnus Dei.

Laurel: The laurel is usually depicted in the form of a wreath and is usually intended to represent victory over death. This likely originated from the tradition in Ancient Rome of crowning winners of contests with laurel wreathes as a sign of their victory and immortality.

Lily: The lily is used as a symbol of chastity and purity. The simple foliage and spectacular flowers are also indicative of a worthy life spent casting off earthly things and investing instead in spiritual wealth.

Morning Glory: Since each flower of the morning glory only lasts for one day, opening in the morning and wilting in the evening, the flower is used to signify the brevity of life. Since the dead flowers are replaced with new flowers the next morning, it is also considered to symbolise the Resurrection.

Olive tree: On its own the olive tree is a sign of peace. In the context of the cemetery, reference to an olive tree is often made by an image of a dove holding an olive branch in its beak, meaning the soul of the deceased had departed in the peace of God. The Bible inspired this symbol in the story of Noah and the Flood when Noah sent out a dove from the ark to look for dry land. Genesis 8:11 recorded the result: 'When the dove returned to him in the evening, there in its beak was a freshly plucked olive leaf! Then Noah knew that the water had receded from the earth.'

Palms: The Romans traditionally regarded palm fronds as a symbol of victory. This was adapted by Christians to mean victory over death and is a common sight in churches at Easter time on Palm Sunday to commemorate Christ's resurrection after the crucifixion.

Poppy: In the Middle Ages, Christians considered the poppy to have similar properties as ears of corn (symbol of fertility and rebirth) because poppies often grew alongside corn. Since World War I (1914–18), the poppy symbolises the soldiers killed in the fields of Flanders in France and wreathes of red paper poppies are placed at military graves in the cemetery on Remembrance Sunday each November.

Rose: The beauty and rich fragrance of the rose has long been associated with decadence and self-indulgence and was originally disregarded by Christians. However, the flower's widespread and enduring popularity eventually resulted in it being included as a Christian symbol — a red rose representing martyrdom and a white rose representing purity. Thorny roses were only to be found on earth symbolising the sin of the world while the sweet fragrance gave a foretaste of what Heaven would be like. In the Victorian era, roses were often used to decorate women's graves.

Thistle: As well as identifying the deceased's nationality as Scottish, the prickly thistle is associated with earthly sorrow (similar to the Acanthus) and the crown of thorns worn by Christ at his crucifixion. In Genesis 3:18, God banishes Adam and Eve from the Garden of Eden cursing the land and saying to Adam: 'Thorns also and thistles shall it bring forth to thee, and thou shalt eat the herb of the field.'

Hand

A hand that points up indicates that the soul of the deceased has risen heavenward. Since hands and extended arms of carved angels are vulnerable to breakage, it is important that maintenance teams ensure repairs do not inadvertently replace the limbs pointing downwards. Two hands placed together, as if shaking, usually symbolise marriage. If the hands do not display obvious differences in gender, then the handshake is more likely to represent a fond farewell from earth or a friendly welcome to heaven. A hand that is shown reaching down from Heaven is the hand of God. In cemeteries, the right hand is used to symbolise God's blessing. The left hand would be a sign of God's curse.

Masonic symbols

All-seeing eye: This is an ancient symbol for God comprising an eye within a triangle and often includes radiating rays of light. The symbol is used by many different cultures with both good and bad connotations. In a cemetery it always means the deceased was a mason (a member of a large and secretive fraternal organisation).

Square and compass: This symbol and variations of it show that the deceased was a mason. The draughting instruments represent the interaction between mind and matter and refer to the masons' belief in the logical progression from the material to the intellectual and the spiritual. Common variations include a 'G' in between the square and compass that has been said to stand for either 'Geometry' or 'God' depending upon your point of view. Clasped hands are sometimes included (see Hand's description above).

Rock

A rock signifies stability, reliability and strength. There are many references to these qualities in the Bible, e.g., Psalm 18:2: 'The Lord is my rock, and my fortress.' Christ also refers to his disciple Peter as a cornerstone of the church in Matthew 16:18: 'Upon this rock I will build my church, and the gates of hell shall not prevail against it.'

Ship

The worldly significance of an entire ship motif is usually that the deceased was a sailor and went down with the ship. The religious symbolism would be associated with Noah's ark and the protective properties of a large ship weathering a storm. The masts of a sailing ship have the added symbolism of the cross.

Symbols of the Passion

Symbols that show events leading up to and immediately following Christ's crucifixion are known as symbols of the Passion. Some of the most common ones found on headstones include: a cross above a chalice (the setting of Gethsemane or 'Garden of Tears' where Judas betrayed Jesus); hammer and nails (the crucifixion); an empty cross with nails and the letters INRI (descent from the cross).

ΑΩ: Alpha and Omega are the first and last letters of the Greek alphabet and are significant symbols in Christian cemeteries to represent the beginning and end of all things (Revelations 21:6): 'He said to me: "It is done. I am the Alpha and the Omega, the Beginning and the End." ' If the Greek letter M (Mu) is inserted between the Alpha and Omega, it means the beginning, the continuation, and the end of all things.

Chalice: The chalice is symbolic of the cup (or holy grail) of wine given by Christ at the Last Supper to the disciples and said to have been used to collect Christ's blood at the foot of the cross. Communion or Eucharist ceremonies recreate the scene of the Last Supper by administering wine in a chalice to the congregation with Christ's words (Mark 14:24): 'And he said unto them, "This is my blood of the covenant which is poured out for many." '

IHS and IHC: These are also commonly carved onto crosses. IHS is derived from the first three letters of Jesus' name using the Greek alphabet (*Iota, Eta, Sigma*) and IHC is the equivalent using the Roman alphabet.

INRI: This monogram is often found carved onto crosses and comprises the first letters of the Latin words *Iesus Nazarenus Rex Iudaeorum* or 'Jesus of Nazareth, King of the Jews'.

Nails: Nails are fairly obvious symbols being associated with the crucifixion. Normally three nails are shown to represent the Trinity.

Pax: *Pax* is the Latin word for 'peace' and can be abbreviated to PX.

RIP: These are the most common letters found on headstones and is an abbreviation of the Latin *Requiescat In Pace* or 'Rest in Peace.'

References

The following references have been very helpful in compiling this glossary of cemetery icons.

Chevalier J., and A. Gheerbrant. 1996. *The Penguin Dictionary of Symbols.*London: Penguin Books.

Keister, D. 2004. *Stories in Stone: A Field Guide to Cemetery Symbolism and Iconography.* Salt Lake City: Gibbs Smith.

Maxwell, I., R. Nanda, and D. Urquhart. 2001. *Guide for Practitioners 2: Conservation of Historic Graveyards.* Edinburgh: Historic Scotland.

Willsher, B. 1996. Scottish *Epitaphs: Epitaphs and Images from Scottish Graveyards.* Edinburgh: Canongate Books Ltd.

———. 1995. *Understanding Scottish Graveyards.* Edinburgh: W. & R. Chambers Ltd.

Appendix 2

Cemetery Tree and Palm Species and Their Use by Fauna

Trees and Palms	Use by Fauna	Trees and Palms	Use by Fauna
Albizia lebbeck (Lebbeck tree)		**Gordonia axillaris** (Gordonia)	M/N
Aleurites moluccana (Candlenut tree)		**Juniperus chinensis** (Chinese juniper)	
Araucaria heterophylla (Norfolk Island pine)		**Leucaena leucocephala** (White popinac)	
Archontophoenix alexandrae (King palm, Alexandra palm)	BT	**Ligustrum japonicum** (Japanese privet)	BD/M/N
Bauhinia blakeana (Hong Kong orchid tree)	BD/M	**Litchi chinensis** (Lychee)	BT/M/F
Bauhinia purpurea (Purple camel's foot tree)	BD/M/N	**Litsea glutinosa** (Pond spice)	M
Bauhinia variegata (Camel's foot tree)	BD/M	**Litsea monopetala** (Persimmon-leaved litsea)	
Bombax malabaricum (Cotton tree)	BT/BD	**Livistona chinensis** (Chinese fan palm)	DFFB/BD
Canarium album (Chinese white olive)		**Macaranga tanarius** (Elephant's ear)	BD/M
Canthium dicoccum (Green coffee tree)		**Machilus chinensis** (Hong Kong machilus)	BD/M
Cassia siamea (Kassod tree)		**Magnolia grandiflora** (Lotus-flowered magnolia)	
Casuarina equisetifolia (Horsetail tree)		**Mallotus paniculatus** (Turn-in-the-wind)	BD/M
Celtis sinensis (Chinese hackberry)	BD/M	**Mangifera indica** (Mango)	M/F

Trees and Palms	Use by Fauna	Trees and Palms	Use by Fauna
Celtis timorensis (Hackberry)		Melaleuca quinquenervia (Paperbark tree)	
Chrysalidocarpus lutescens (Bamboo palm)		Michelia alba (White champak)	
Cinnamomum burmanii (Cinnamon tree)	BD	Microcos paniculata (Microcos)	M
Cinnamomum camphora (Camphor tree)	BD/M	Phoenix roebelenii (Dwarf date-palm)	BD
Cinnamomum parthenoxylon (Yellow camphor tree)		Pinus massoniana (Chinese red pine)	
Clausena lansium (Wampi)		Plumeria rubra var. acutifolia (Frangipani)	
Cleistocalyx operculata (Water banyan)	M	Psidium guajava (Guava)	DFFB/M/F
Crateva unilocularis (Spider tree, Gold-and-silver tree)	M	Sapium discolor (Mountain tallow)	BD/M
Cratoxylum ligustrinum (Yellow cow wood)	M	Schefflera octophylla (Ivy tree)	BT/BD/M/N
Delonix regia (Flame of the forest)	M/N	Scolopia chinensis (Chinese scolopia)	M
Eucalyptus citriodora (Lemon-scented gum)	B/T	Scolopia saeva (Scolopia)	
Euphoria longan (Longan)	M/F	Sterculia lanceolata (Scarlet sterculia)	M
Eurya japonica (Eurya)	BD	Swietenia mahogani (West Indies mahogany)	
Ficus microcarpa (Chinese banyan)	BT/MPC/BD/M/F	Syzygium jambos (Rose-apple)	BT/BD/M/F
Ficus variegata var. chlorocarpa (Common red-stem fig)	BT/MPC	Syzygium samarangense (Java-apple)	M
Ficus virens var. sublanceolata (Big-leaved fig)	BT/MPC/BD	Vitex quinata (Wild vitex)	DFFB

Garcinia oblongifolia
(Wild mangosteen)

Washingtonia robusta
(Petticoat palm)

Glyptostrobus pensilis
(Water pine)

Key to 'Use by Fauna'	
BD	BIRDS
BF	BUTTERFLIES (important host plant for larvae)
BT	BATS
DFFB	DOG-FACED FRUIT BATS
F	FRUIT (over-ripe: food source for M/BF)
M	MOTHS
MPC	MASKED PALM CIVETS
N	NECTAR (for M/BF adults)

Source: Tree and palm species surveyed and identified by author, 'Use by Fauna' advised by Dr Gary Ades and Dr Roger Kendrick of Kadoorie Farm and Botanical Garden.

Appendix 3

Butterfly and Moth Species Recorded in the Cemetery (1 October 2004)

Butterflies	Moths
Graphium sarpedon	Edosa species
Papilio polytes	Strathmopoda xanthomochla
Papilio protenor	Odites ricinella
Catopsilia pomona	Helcystogramma triannulella
Eurema hecabe	Chlidanotinae genus and species ✔
Hebomoia glaucippe	Cryptaspasma helota
Cupha erymanthis	Sorolopha archimedias
Euthalia phemius	Pseudargyria interruptella
Euthalia lubentina	Cnaphalocrocis medinalis
Euploea midamus	Eurrhyparodes bracteolalis
Ideopsis similis	Herpetogramma licarsisalis
Mycalesis mineus	Herpetogramma submarginalis
Chilades pandava	Hydriris ornatalis
Jamides bochus	Metasia coniotalis
Neopithecops zalmora	Spoladea recurvalis
Zizeeria maha	Herculia negrivitta
Abisara echerius	Macroglossum pyrrhosticta
Zemeros flegyas	Artaxa species ✔
Hyarotis adrastus	Orgyia postica

Photo of rare Chlidanotinae

Eressa confines

Condica conducta

Metaemene atriguttata

Gesonia obeiditalis

Lophoptera squammigera

Hydrillodes abavalis

Nodaria externalis

Spodoptera cilium

Spodoptera litura

(✔ denotes rare species, only recorded on two to four previous occasions)

Source: Hong Kong Lepidopterist Society: butterfly list by Yiu Vor, moth list by Roger Kendrick, photo of rare moth by Byron Li.

Notes

1 Grave Concerns

1. Samuel Johnson, *Rasselas, Prince of Abissinia* (London: Edward Lacey, 1838), 4.

2. *The History of Rasselas, Prince of Abissinia*, often abbreviated to *Rasselas*, is a novella written by Dr Samuel Johnson in January 1759 to raise money to support his sick mother. Dr Johnson was one of England's greatest literary critics, poets and essayists. He was also responsible for the Herculean task of compiling the first English dictionary.

3. James Bodell, *A Soldier's View of Empire: The Reminiscences of James Bodell, 1831–92,* edited by Keith Sinclair (London: Bodley Head, 1982), 66.

4. W. F. Mayers et al., *The Treaty Ports of China and Japan* (London: Trübner & Co., 1867), 12–13.

5. Hong Kong Government, *Historical and Statistical Abstract of the Colony of Hong Kong 1841–1930* (Hong Kong: Government Printer, 1932), 4.

6. Henry Knollys, *English Life in China* (London: Smith Elder & Co., 1885), 18.

7. Ibid., 20.

8. Sydney B. Skertchly, *Our Island: A Naturalist's Description of Hong Kong* (Hong Kong: Kelly and Walsh, 1893), 49, and James J. Walker, 'A Preliminary List of the Butterflies of Hong Kong; based on Observations and Captures made during the Winter and Spring Months of 1892 and 1893', *Transactions of the Entomological Society of London* Part IV (December 1895): 439.

9. J. C. Kershaw, *Butterflies of Hong Kong and South-East China* (Hong Kong: Kelly and Walsh, 1907), Prefaratory.

10. Hong Kong Government, *Colonial Office Report* (Hong Kong: Hong Kong Government, 1911), 110.

11. Bard, Solomon M., *Study of Military Graves and Monuments: Hong Kong Cemetery* (Hong Kong: Antiquities and Monuments Office, 1991), 7.

12. Ibid., 45.

2 Origins of the Cemetery Garden

1. Judi Culbertson and Tom Randall, *Permanent Parisians: An Illustrated, Biographical Guide to the Cemeteries of Paris* (London: Robson Books, 2000), 7.
2. William Blake, *Milton* (1804). Reprint, David Bindman editor, *Blake's Illuminated Books*, vol. 5 (London: Tate Gallery, 1991).
3. F. Krupa, 'Paris: Urban Sanitation Before the 20th Century' [Online]. Available from http://www.op.net/~uarts/krupa/alltextparis.html.
4. Ibid.
5. Ibid.
6. Judi Culbertson and Tom Randall, *Permanent Parisians*, 8.
7. Richard A. Etlin, 'Pere Lachaise and the Garden Cemetery', *Journal of Garden History*, Vol. 4, No. 3 (1984): 219.
8. Response to questionnaire by Monsieur Christian Charlet (Paris Cemetery Department Historian), 24 December 2004.
9. Brent Elliot, 'The Landscape of the English Cemetery', *Landscape Design* (October 1989): 13.
10. Ibid.
11. James Stevens Curl, A *Celebration of Death: An Introduction to Some of the Buildings, Monuments, and Settings of Funerary Architecture in the Western European Tradition* (London: B. T. Batsford Ltd., 1993), 210.
12. James J. Berry, *The Glasgow Necropolis Heritage Trail and Historical Account* (Glasgow: Glasgow City Council).
13. Ibid.
14. John Strang, *Necropolis Glasguensis with Observations on Ancient and Modern Tombs and Sepulture* (Glasgow: Merchant's House of Glasgow, 1831), 28.
15. James J. Berry, *The Glasgow Necropolis.*
16. Ibid.
17. Ibid.
18. James Steven Curl, 'The Design of the Early British Cemeteries', *Journal of Garden History*, Vol. 4, No. 3 (1984): 232.
19. John C. Loudon, *On the Laying Out, Planting and Managing of Cemeteries and on the Improvement of Churchyards* (Redhill: Ivelet Books Ltd., 1981), 13.
20. Brent Elliot, 'The Landscape of the English Cemetery', 13.
21. Ibid.
22. John C. Loudon, *On the Laying Out, Planting and Managing of Cemeteries*, 70.
23. James Steven Curl, *A Celebration of Death*, 263.
24. Mike Dash, *Tulipomania* (New York: Three Rivers Press, 2000), 9–10.
25. Ibid., 10.
26. John C. Loudon, *On the Laying Out, Planting and Managing of Cemeteries*, 70.
27. Ibid., 22.

28. Ibid., 56.
29. Brent Elliot, 'The Landscape of the English Cemetery', 13–4.
30. James J. Berry, *The Glasgow Necropolis*.
31. Protest slogan against the proposed closure of the urban cemeteries, Paris late 1800s.
32. James J. Berry, *The Glasgow Necropolis*.
33. Ibid.
34. Julie Rugg and Julie Dunk, 'Conserving Cemeteries', *Landscape Design* (November 1994): 26.
35. Ibid., 25.

3 The Rise and Fall of the Hong Kong Cemetery

1. John Strang, *Necropolis Glasguensis with Observations on Ancient and Modern Tombs and Sepulture* (Glasgow: Merchant's House of Glasgow, 1831), 62.
2. Hal Empson, *Mapping Hong Kong* (Hong Kong: Government Printer, 1992), 130.
3. Geotechnical Engineering Office, *Geological Survey of Hong Kong and Kowloon* (Sheet 11, Series HGM20, Edition 1-1986).
4. Jason Wordie, 'Walking Tour Notes: The Colonial (Hong Kong) Cemetery'.
5. G. B. Endacott, *A History of Hong Kong* (Hong Kong: Oxford University Press, 1973), 68.
6. Jason Wordie, 'Walking Tour Notes'.
7. John C. Loudon, *On the Laying Out, Planting and Managing of Cemeteries and on the Improvement of Churchyards* (Redhill: Ivelet Books Ltd., 1981), 6.
8. Ibid., 14.
9. Solomon M. Bard, *Garrison Memorials in Hong Kong: Some Graves and Monuments at Happy Valley* (Hong Kong: Antiquities and Monuments Office, 1997), 26.
10. Article in *China Mail*, 23 November 1865.
11. Carl T. Smith, 'Notes for a Visit to the Government Cemetery at Happy Valley', *Journal of the Hong Kong Branch of the Royal Asiatic Society* Vol. 25 (1985): 18.
12. Article in *China Mail*, 23 November 1865.
13. Carl T. Smith, 'Notes for a Visit to the Government Cemetery at Happy Valley', 18.
14. Jason Wordie, 'Walking Tour Notes'.
15. Solomon M. Bard, *Garrison Memorials in Hong Kong*, 126.
16. Brent Elliot, 'The Landscape of the English Cemetery', *Landscape Design* (October 1989): 13.

17. Charles Ford, 'Report of the Botanical and Forestry Department', *Administrative Report* 1883 (Hong Kong: Government Publications, 1883), para. 7.

18. W. J. Tutcher, 'Report of the Botanical and Forestry Department', *Administrative Report* 1910 (Hong Kong: Government Publications, 1910), L2.

19. W. J. Tutcher, 'Report of the Botanical and Forestry Department', *Administrative Report* 1911 (Hong Kong: Government Publications, 1911), M3.

20. LCSD website: http://ovt.lcsd.gov.hk

21. Interview with Mr Fukumitsu, Secretary General of the Hong Kong Japanese Club, 23 December 2004.

22. Interviews with Cemetery Managers of Muslim, Catholic and Parsee Cemeteries, September to November 2004.

23. Article entitled 'Lest We Forget' in *South China Morning Post*, 6 June 1913.

24. Lau Chu-pak, quoted in *Weekly Press*, 17 April 1909.

25. Hong Kong Government, *Colonial Office Report* (Hong Kong: Hong Kong Government, 1911), 110.

26. Ibid.

27. Carl T. Smith, 'Notes for a Visit to the Government Cemetery at Happy Valley', 19.

28. Ibid.

29. Ibid., 23.

30. Ibid., 18.

31. Correspondence between Mr R. J. C. Howes of the Colonial Secretariat and the Dean of St. John's Cathedral on 28 October 1954, responding to the Dean's query regarding the official stance on eligibility for burial at the Hong Kong Cemetery.

32. Solomon M. Bard, *Study of Military Graves and Monuments: Hong Kong Cemetery* (Hong Kong: Antiquities and Monuments Office, 1991), 45.

33. Interview with FEHD staff of Hong Kong Cemetery, June 2004.

34. J. C. Kershaw, *Butterflies of Hong Kong and South-East China* (Hong Kong: Kelly and Walsh, 1907), Prefatory.

35. James J. Walker, 'A Preliminary List of the Butterflies of Hong Kong; based on Observations and Captures made during the Winter and Spring Months of 1892 and 1893', *Transactions of the Entomological Society of London* Part IV (December 1895): 439.

36. Sydney B. Skertchly, *Our Island: A Naturalist's Description of Hong Kong* (Hong Kong: Kelly and Walsh, 1893), 49.

37. Conversation with Dr Roger Kendrick and Mr Yiu Vor, members of the Hong Kong Lepidopterist Society, 6 January 2005.

4 Self-guided Tour

1. John C. Loudon, *On the Laying Out, Planting and Managing of Cemeteries and on the Improvement of Churchyards* (Redhill: Ivelet Books Ltd., 1981), 13.
2. Edward H. Cree, Naval Surgeon: *The Voyages of Dr Edward H. Cree, Royal Navy* (New York: Dutton, 1981), 90 (copyright of illustration: 1981 by Dorys Annette Cree).
3. The following references would make excellent further reading and have been helpful in describing the colourful characters highlighted on the tour and historical background to the cemetery in general.

   Bard, Solomon M. 1997. *Garrison Memorials in Hong Kong: Some Graves and Monuments at Happy Valley*. Hong Kong: Antiquities and Monuments Office.
   Eitel, E. J. 1895. *Europe in China: The History of Hongkong from the Beginning to the Year* 1882. Hong Kong: Kelly and Walsh.
   Endacott, G. B. 1973. *A History of Hong Kong*. Hong Kong: Oxford University Press.
   ———. 2005. *A Biographical Sketch-book of Early Hong Kong*. Hong Kong: Hong Kong University Press.
   Smith, Carl T. 1985. 'Notes for a Visit to the Government Cemetery at Happy Valley', *Journal of the Hong Kong Branch of the Royal Asiatic Society*, Vol. 25: 19.

5 Last Words

1. Home Affairs Bureau, *Review of Built Heritage Conservation Policy: Consultation   Document* (Hong Kong: Hong Kong Government, 2004), 15.
2. Returned questionnaire from Père Lachaise Management Staff, 24 December 2004.
3. Returned questionnaire from Glasgow Necropolis Management Staff, 23 June 2004.
4. Interviews with Managers of Muslim, Catholic and Parsee Cemeteries, September through November 2004.
5. Returned questionnaire from Glasgow Necropolis Management Staff, 23 June 2004.

6. I. Maxwell, R. Nanda and D. Urquhart, *Guide for Practitioners 2: Conservation of Historic Graveyards* (Edinburgh: Historic Scotland, 2001). See also T. Anson-Cartwright, ed., *Landscape of Memories: A Guide for Conserving Historic Cemeteries, Repairing Tombstones* (Ontario: Ministry of Citizenship, Culture and Recreation, 1998).
7. Julie Rugg and Julie Dunk, 'Conserving Cemeteries', *Landscape Design* (November 1994): 25–26.
8. Carl T. Smith, 'Notes for a Visit to the Government Cemetery at Happy Valley', *Journal of the Hong Kong Branch of the Royal Asiatic Society* Vol. 25 (1985): 19.
9. Article in the *China Mail*, 23 November 1865.

Index

Note: The page number is in bold if it refers to an illustration.

136

INDEX